# Personal Privacy

# PERSONAL PRIVACY

## VITA CORNELIUS (EDITOR)

**Novinka Books**
*New York*

**Senior Editors:** Susan Boriotti and Donna Dennis
**Coordinating Editor:** Tatiana Shohov
**Office Manager:** Annette Hellinger
**Graphics:** Wanda Serrano
**Editorial Production:** Jennifer Vogt, Matthew Kozlowski, Jonathan Rose
and Maya Columbus
**Circulation:** Ave Maria Gonzalez, Indah Pecker, Raymond Davis,
Vladimir Klestov and Jonathan Roque
**Communications and Acquisitions:** Serge P. Shohov
**Marketing:** Cathy DeGregory

*Library of Congress Cataloging-in-Publication Data*
*Available Upon Request*

ISBN: 1-59033-230-X.

Copyright © 2002 by Novinka Books
Nova Science Publishers, Inc.
227 Main Street, Suite 100
Huntington, New York 11743
Tele. 631-424-NOVA (6682)     Fax 631-425-5933
E Mail: Novascience@earthlink.net
www.novapublishers.com

All rights reserved. No part of this book may be reproduced, stored in a retrieval system or transmitted in any form or by any means: electronic, electrostatic, magnetic, tape, mechanical photocopying, recording or otherwise without permission from the publishers.

The publisher has taken reasonable care in the preparation of this book, but makes no expressed or implied warranty of any kind and assumes no responsibility for any errors or omissions. No liability is assumed for incidental or consequential damages in connection with or arising out of information contained in this book.

This publication is designed to provide accurate and authoritative information with regard to the subject matter covered herein. It is sold with the clear understanding that the publisher is not engaged in rendering legal or any other professional services. If legal or any other expert assistance is required, the services of a competent person should be sought. FROM A DECLARATION OF PARTICIPANTS JOINTLY ADOPTED BY A COMMITTEE OF THE AMERICAN BAR ASSOCIATION AND A COMMITTEE OF PUBLISHERS.

*Printed in the United States of America*

# CONTENTS

| | |
|---|---|
| **Preface** | vii |
| **Personal Privacy Protection: The Legislative Response**<br>*Harold C. Relyea* | 1 |
|     An Evolving Value | 1 |
|     Legislating Privacy Protection | 6 |
|     Privacy Issues before Congress | 28 |
|     For Further Reading | 48 |
| **The Fourth Amendment – A Changing Landscape**<br>*Elizabeth B. Bazan* | 51 |
|     Introduction | 51 |
|     Investigative Stops | 55 |
|     Police Questioning and Luggage Search on a Bus | 56 |
|     Sobriety Checkpoints | 58 |
|     Chasing a Fleeing Suspect | 60 |
|     Use of Excessive or Deadly Force | 60 |
|     Detention before Probable Cause Hearing | 64 |
|     Aerial Searches | 65 |
|     Plain View Exception to Warrant Requirement | 66 |
|     Evidence in Plain View Discovered During Protective Sweep of House-- Scope of Protective Sweep | 68 |
|     Warrantless Routine In-Home Arrest | 69 |
|     Impeachment Exception to Exclusionary Rule | 69 |
|     Searches of Closed Containers in Vehicles | 70 |
|     Employee Drug-Testing | 74 |
|     Fourth Amendment Extra-Territorial Application | 74 |
|     Conclusions | 74 |
| **Index** | 77 |

# PREFACE

The notion of personal privacy has been long present in American society. The Bill of Rights gave constitutional recognition to several privacy aspects, including the first amendment's freedom of expression and association. However, not to be overlooked are prohibitions against quartering troops in private homes, unwarranted searches and seizures, and self-incrimination. Despite significant ambiguity about many the aspects of personal privacy, Americans have turned increasingly to Congress for safeguarding their liberties. This book presents a select overlook of personal privacy in America, its continual evolution, and its impact on society.

# PERSONAL PRIVACY PROTECTION: THE LEGISLATIVE RESPONSE

*Harold C. Relyea*

An expectation of personal privacy seemingly has long prevailed in American culture and society. Some may regard personal privacy as one of the "Blessings of Liberty" mentioned in the preamble of the Constitution. Others might trace its roots to the "right of the people to be secure in their persons, houses, papers, and effects" given expression in the Fourth Amendment of that document. Although there may be some ambiguity about all of the facets of personal privacy, the American people, particularly during the latter half of the 20$^{th}$ century, have increasingly turned to Congress to respond to their concerns regarding perceived threats to, or the loss of, personal privacy. These responses, which have significantly contributed to the policy development of the personal privacy concept, are reviewed here, and current personal privacy issues receiving legislative treatment are identified and discussed.

## AN EVOLVING VALUE

The concept of privacy has probably long been a value of humankind. As a sentiment—the wish not to be intruded upon—it very likely predates recorded history and was experienced before it was given a name. In the thinking of the influential 17$^{th}$ century British philosopher John Locke, privacy was one of the presocietal or "natural rights" which was preserved when individuals, by social contract, agreed to form a society. Furthermore, when society, by a second social contract, agreed to form a government, privacy was one of the rights the government was expected to preserve and protect. When a Bill of Rights was appended to the American version of Locke's second contract, it gave constitutional recognition to privacy expectations in the First Amendment, including the right not to have to speak, privacy of opinion, freedom of association, and the right of anonymous or pseudonymous expression; the Third Amendment, prohibiting the quartering of troops in private homes during peacetime without the owner's consent; the Fourth Amendment, guaranteeing personal security against unwarranted searches and seizures; and the Fifth Amendment, specifying the privilege against self-incrimination.[1] In a landmark 1965 decision, the Supreme Court viewed these and the Ninth Amendment as being the sources of a penumbral right of privacy.[2]

In his seminal study of privacy, attorney Alan F. Westin has written that American society, prior to the Civil War, "had a thorough and effective set of rules with which to protect individual and group privacy from the means of compulsory disclosure and physical surveillance known in that era."[3] Toward the cud of the 19$^{th}$ century, new technology—the telephone, the microphone and dictograph recorder, and improved cameras—presented major new challenges to privacy protection. Consequently, understandings of privacy became a bit desperate, Judge Thomas Cooley, in his influential treatise on torts, described privacy as the inalienable and natural "right to be let alone."[4] This view was given more popular expression by Samuel D. Warren and Louis D. Brandeis in their now famous 1890 *Harvard Law Review* article on the right to privacy.[5] However, as a British study committee observed in 1972, this perspective "turns out on closer examination to go so far beyond any right which the individual living in an organized society could reasonably claim, that it would be useless as a basis for the granting of legal protection. Any law which proclaimed this as a

---

[1] Alan F. Westin, *Privacy and Freedom* (New York: Atheneum, 1970), pp. 330-333.
[2] *Griswold* v. *Connecticut,* 381 U.S. 479 (1965); see R. H. Clark, "Constitutional Sources of the Penumbral Right to Privacy," *Villunova LawReview,* vol. 19, June 1974, pp. 833-884.
[3] Westin, *Privacy and Freedom,* pp. 337-338.
[4] Thomas M. Cooley, A Treatise on the Law of Torts, or the Wrongs Which Arise Independent of Contract (Chicago: Callaghan and Company, 1888), p. 29.
[5] Samuel D. Warren and Louis D. Brandeis, "The Right to Privacy," *Harvard Law Review,* vol. 4, Dec. *15,* 1890, pp. 193-220.

general right," the committee reported, "would have to qualify the right in so many ways that the generality of the concept would be destroyed."[6]

Nonetheless, new technology would continue to threaten and weaken personal privacy. In 1956, sociologist Edward A. Shils described privacy as "the voluntary withholding of information reinforced by a willing indifference."[7] By that time, however, it had become quite apparent to many that it was increasingly difficult and, in some cases, probably impossible to voluntarily withhold personal information any longer because there were elements of society which had obviously forsaken a willing indifference to such desires.

A few years later, Congress began to probe a variety of privacy issues. For example, in 1965, one subcommittee of the Senate Committee on the Judiciary began omnibus hearings on the invasion of privacy by federal agencies,[8] while a companion subcommittee examined psychological testing procedures and the rights of federal employees.[9] The following year, this latter panel explored the privacy rights of federal civil servants.[10] Another subcommittee began major hearings in 1967 concerning privacy protection by prohibiting wire interception and eavesdropping.[11] It also scrutinized computer privacy that same year.[12] In 1969, Senate subcommittee attention

---

[6] United Kingdom, Committee on Privacy, *Report of the Committee on Privacy* (London: Her Majesty's Stationery Office, 1972), p. 10. The committee was chaired by Kenneth Younger.
[7] Edward A. Shils, *The Torment of Secrecy* (New York Free Press, *1956)*, p. 26.
[8] See U.S. Congress, Senate Committee on the Judiciary, Subcommittee on Administrative Practice and Procedure, *Invasions of Privacy*, hearings, 89th Cong., 1st and 2nd sess., 1965-1966 (Washington: GPO, 1965-1967), 6 parts.
[9] See U.S. Congress, Senate Committee on the Judiciary, Subcommittee on Constitutional Rights, *Psychological Tests and Constitutional Rights*, hearings, 89th Cong., 1st sess., June 7-10, 1965 (Washington: GPO, 1966).
[10] See U.S. Congress, Senate Committee on the Judiciary, Subcommittee on Constitutional Rights, *Privacy and the Rights of Federal Employees*, hearings, 89th Cong., 2nd sess., Oct. 3-5, 1966 (Washington: GPO, 1966).
[11] See U.S. Congress, Senate Committee on the Judiciary, Subcommittee on Administrative Practice and Procedure, *Right of Privacy Act of 1967*, hearings, 90th Cong., 1st sess., Mar. 20; Apr. 4-6, 19-21; May 17-19, 1967 (Washington: GPO, 1967), 2 parts.
[12] See U.S. Congress, Senate Committee on the Judiciary, Subcommittee on Administrative Practice and Procedure, *Computer Privacy*, hearings, 90the Cong., 1st and 2nd sess., Mar. 14-15, 1967; Feb. 6, 1968 (Washington: GPO, 1967-1968), 2 parts.

was given to privacy, the census, and federal questionnaires.[13] In 1971, omnibus hearings were held on federal databanks, computers, and the Bill of Rights.[14] In the House, the Committee on Government Operations (now Government Reform) chartered a Special Subcommittee on Invasion of Privacy in 1965.[15] It launched a general inquiry that year,[16] then focused upon the computer and invasion of privacy the following year,[17] and was a major critic of a proposed national databank under discussion in the 1960s.[18] In 1968, a subcommittee of the House Committee on Post Office and Civil Service examined privacy and the rights of federal employees.[19] That same year, the special subcommittee explored the practices of commercial credit bureaus and their privacy implications.[20] In 1972, a subcommittee on the House Committee on the Judiciary held hearings on the security and privacy of criminal arrest records.[21]

In 1968, at the urging of Alan F. Westin, the Russell Sage Foundation funded the Project on Computer Databanks of the Computer Science and Engineering Board, National Academy of Sciences. This undertaking, directed by Westin, examined the use of computers by government and private organizations for collecting, processing, and exchanging information about individuals; the effect of such computer use on the way organizations utilize records in order to make judgments about rights, benefits, and

---

[13] See U.S. Congress, Senate Committee on the Judiciary, Subcommittee on Constitutional Rights, *Privacy, the Census* and Federal *Questionnaires,* hearings 91$^{st}$ Cong., 1$^{st}$ sess., Apr. 24-25; May 2; July 1, 1969 (Washington: GPO, 1969).

[14] See U.S. Congress, Senate Committee on the Judiciary, Subcommittee on Constitutional Rights, *Federal Data Banks, Computers and the Bill of Rights,* hearings, 92$^{nd}$ Cong., 1$^{st}$ sess., Feb. 23-25; Mar. 2-4, 9-11, 15, 17, 1971 (Washington: GPO, 1971), 2 parts.

[15] See Morris S. Ogul, *Congress Oversees the Bureaucracy* (Pittsburgh: University of Pittsburgh Press, 1976), pp. 92-128.

[16] See U.S. Congress, House Committee on Government Operations, *Special Inquiry on Invasion of Privacy,* hearing, 89$^{th}$ Cong., 1$^{st}$ sess., June 2-4, 7, 23; Sept. 23, 1965; May 24, 1966 (Washington: GPO, 1966), 2 parts.

[17] See U.S. Congress, House Committee on Government Operations, *The Computer and Invasion of Privacy,* hearing, 89$^{th}$ Cong., 2$^{nd}$ sess., June 26-28, 1966 (Washington: GPO, 1966).

[18] See U.S. Congress, House Committee on Government Operations, *Privacy and the National Data Bank Concept, 9$^{th}$* Cong., 2$^{nd}$ sess., H. Rept. 1842 (Washington: GPO, 1968).

[19] See U.S. Congress, House Committee on Post Office and Civil Service, *Privacy and the Rights of Federal Employees,* hearings, 9$^{th}$ Cong., 2$^{nd}$ sess., June 13, 18, 27; July 2, 9-12, 16-17, 1968 (Washington: GPO, 1968).

[20] See U.S. Congress, House Committee on Government Operations, *Commercial Credit Bureaus,* hearings, 9$^{th}$ Cong., 2$^{nd}$ sess Mar. 12-14, 1968 (Washington: GPO, 1968).

[21] See U.S. Congress, House Committee on the Judiciary, *Security and Privacy of Criminal Arrest Records,* hearings, 92$^{nd}$ cong., 2$^{nd}$ sess., ar. 16, 22-23; Apr. 13, 26, 1972 (Washington: GPO, 1972).

opportunities of individuals; and the impact of computerized records systems on privacy and due process rules. In the final report, published in 1972, the Project found that "computer usage has not created the revolutionary new powers of data surveillance predicted by some commentators"; that some important increases in the efficiency of organizational record-keeping resulted from computerization; and that, "even where these increases in efficiency are taking place, organizational policies which affect individual rights are still generally following the pre-computer patters in each field of record-keeping."[22]

The report, however, was not satisfied with a pattern of organizations merely adapting their computerized systems of record-keeping to the existing civil liberties rules in their particular fields. Thus, it recommended that compulsory data collection be limited "so that matters that ought not to be considered in making decisions about individuals do not become part of the formal records at all"; that individuals be given greater rights of access to records maintained about them; and that "new rules for data sharing and confidentiality ... be fashioned."[23]

Early in 1972, Secretary of Health, Education, and Welfare Elliott L. Richardson established the Secretary's Advisory Committee on Automated Personal Data Systems. Headed by Willis H. Ware of the Rand Corporation, the panel was asked to analyze and make recommendations about four areas of interest.

- Harmful consequences that may result from using automated personal data systems;
- Safeguards that might protect against potentially harmful consequences that may result from using automated personal data systems;
- Measures that might afford redress for any such harmful consequences; and
- Policy and practice relating to the issuance and use of individuals' Social Security numbers.[24]

---

[22] National Academy of Sciences, Computer Science and Engineering Board, Project on Computer Databanks, *Databanks in a Free Society*, Report of the Project on computer Databanks (New York: Quadrangle Books, 1972), p. 341.

[23] *Ibid. pp. 348-349.*

[24] U.S. Department of Health, Education, and Welfare, Secretary's Advisory Committee on Automated Personal Data Systems, *Records, Computers, and the Rights of Citizens* (Washington: July 1973), p. ix.

In its final report, issued in July 1973, the advisory committee recommended "the enactment of legislation establishing a Code of Fair Information Practice for all automated personal data systems." Such a code, in the view of the panel, should "define 'fair information practice' as adherence to specified safeguard requirements"; "prohibit violation of any safeguard requirements as an 'unfair information practice'"; provide that an unfair information practice be subject to both civil and criminal penalties"; "provide for injunctions to prevent violations of any safeguard requirement"; "give individuals the right to bring suits for unfair information practices to recover actual, liquidated, and punitive damages, in individual or class actions"; and "also provide for recovery of reasonable attorneys' fees and other costs of litigation incurred by individuals who bring successful lawsuits.[25]

# LEGISLATING PRIVACY PROTECTION

During the past three decades, Congress has legislated privacy protections in various policy areas and has initiated two broad privacy studies with a view to producing both findings and policy recommendations. Major developments resulting from these initiatives are summarized below.

### Fair Credit Reporting Act

Before the HEW Secretary's Advisory Committee on Automated Personal Data Systems issued its July 1973 final report recommending a Code of Fair Information Practice, Congress experimented with such a set of ground rules when it made an initial effort at legislating a new kind of privacy protection with the Fair Credit Reporting Act of 1970.[26] This statute regulates the collection and dissemination of personal information by consumer reporting agencies and persons, including corporations, who regularly procure or cause to be prepared investigative consumer reports on any individual for use by a third party. Among its provisions, the new law authorized the subject of a consumer report to request of the preparer agency details concerning the nature and scope of all information in its files regarding that individual, the identity of the sources of the information, and

---

[25] *Ibid.*, pp. xxiii and 50.
[26] 84 Stat. 1128; 15 U.S.C. 1681 *et seq.*

the name of any recipient of the information. In addition, the report subject might seek to correct or otherwise amend the preparer agency's information by providing supplemental data.

## Crime Control Act

When legislating the Crime Control Act of 1973, Congress prohibited state agencies receiving law enforcement assistance funds pursuant to the statute and federal personnel from making unauthorized disclosures of personally identifiable criminal history research or statistical information. It also permitted "an individual who believes that criminal history information concerning him contained in an automated system is inaccurate, incomplete, or maintained in violation of this [law] to review such information and to obtain a copy of it for the purpose of challenge or correction."[27]

## Privacy Act

With the Privacy Act of 1974, Congress addressed several aspects of privacy protection.[28] First, it sustained some traditional major privacy principles. For example, an agency shall "maintain no record describing how any individual exercises rights guaranteed by the First Amendment unless expressly authorized by statute or by the individual about whom the record is maintained or unless pertinent to and within the scope of an authorized law enforcement activity."[29]

Second, similar to the Fair Credit Reporting Act, the Privacy Act provides an individual who is a citizen of the United States, or an alien lawfully admitted for permanent residence, with access and emendation arrangements for records maintained on him or her by most, but not all, federal agencies. General exemptions in this regard are provided for systems of records maintained by the Central Intelligence Agency and federal criminal law enforcement agencies.

Third, the statute embodies a number of principles of fair information practice recommended by the HEW Secretary's Advisory Committee on

---

[27] 87 Stat. 197 at 215-216; 42 U.S.C. 3789g.
[28] 88 Stat. 1896; 5 U.S.C. *552a*.
[29] 5 U.S.C. *552a(e)(7)*.

Automated Personal Data Systems. For example, it sets certain conditions concerning the disclosure of personally identifiable information; prescribes requirements for the accounting of certain disclosures of such information; requires agencies to "collect information to the greatest extent practicable directly from the subject individual when the information may result in adverse determinations about an individual's rights, benefits, and privileges under Federal programs"; requires agencies to specify their authority and purposes for collecting personally identifiable information from an individual; requires agencies to "maintain all records which are used by the agency in making any determination about any individual with such accuracy, relevance, timeliness, and completeness as is reasonably necessary to assure fairness to the individual in the determination"; and provides civil and criminal enforcement arrangements.

Recently, in a survey of online privacy protections at federal Web sites, GAO found that 23 of 70 agencies had disclosed personal information gathered from their Web sites to third parties, mostly other agencies. However, at least four agencies were discovered to be sharing such information with private entities—trade organizations, bilateral development banks, product manufacturers, distributors, and retailers. The offending agencies were not identified by GAO. Responding to these findings, some privacy advocates called for updating the Privacy Act to specify privacy protections for Internet visitors to agency Web sites, while others urged better oversight and enforcement of the statute.[30]

## Privacy Study Commission

The statute also mandated the Privacy Protection Study Commission, a temporary, seven-member panel tasked to "make a study of the data banks, automated data processing programs, and information systems of governmental, regional, and private organizations, in order to determine the standards and procedures in force for the protection of personal information."[31] The commission was to "recommend to the President and the Congress the extent, if any, to which the requirements and principles of [the Privacy Act] should be applied to the information practices of [such]

---

[30] Lance Gay, "GAO Finds Agencies Sharing Data of On-line Visitors," *Washington Times*, Sept. 8, 2000, p. A3; U.S. General Accounting Office, *Internet Privacy: Agencies' Efforts to Implement OMB's Privacy Policy*, GAO Report GAO/GGD-00-191 (Washington: Sept. 2000).

[31] 88 Stat.1906.

organizations by legislation, administrative action, or voluntary adoption of such requirements and principles, and report on such other legislative recommendations as it may determine to be necessary to protect the privacy of individuals while meeting the legitimate needs of government and society for information."[32]

The commission began operations in early June 1975 under the leadership of chairman David F. Linowes, a University of Illinois political economist, educator, and corporate executive, and vice chairman Willis H. Ware, the Rand Corporation research scientist who had headed the HIEW Secretary's Advisory Committee on Automated Personal Data Systems.[33] Two years later, in July 1977, the final report of the panel, offering 162 recommendations, was submitted to the President and Congress.[34] In general, the commission urged the establishment of a permanent, independent entity within the federal government to monitor, investigate, evaluate, advise, and offer policy recommendations concerning personal privacy matters; better regulation of the use of mailing lists for commercial purposes; adherence to principles of fair information practice by employers; limited government access to personal records held by a private sector record-keeper through adherence to recognized legal processes; and improved privacy protection for educational records. The panel also recommended the adoption of legislation to apply principles of fair information practice, such as those found in the Privacy Act, to personal information collected and managed by the consumer credit, banking, insurance, and medical care sectors of the U.S. economy.

Congressional response to the commission's report was largely positive, some 200 bills incorporating its recommendations being introduced. However, a concerted effort to enact legislation applying principles of fair information practice to personal information collected and managed by the insurance and medical care industries was stalemated into the final days of the 96th Congress. The opposition was sufficient to discourage a return to such legislative efforts for several years.

President Jimmy Carter appointed a cabinet committee to study the commission's recommendations, and received additional evaluations and supplemental recommendations from an interagency task force, resulting in a

---

[32] *Ibid.*
[33] See David F. Linowes, "The U.S. Privacy Protection *Commission,*" *American Behavioral Scientist,* vol. 26, May-June 1983, pp. *577-590.*
[34] U.S. Privacy Protection Study Commission, *Personal Privacy in an Information Society* (Washington: GPO, 1977).

package of national privacy policy proposals which was sent to Congress on April 2, 1979.³⁵ While these developments were underway, the Carter Administration worked with Congress to produce the Right to Financial Privacy Act of 1978, discussed below. Congress largely deferred action on the President's 1979 package of privacy proposals until 1981, but this effort became moot with President Carter's 1980 electoral defeat for a second term.

## Federal Paperwork Commission

In 1974, Congress also established a temporary, 14-member Commission on Federal Paperwork, giving it a broad mandate to consider a variety of aspects of the collection, processing, dissemination, and management of federal information, including "the ways in which policies and practices relating to the maintenance of confidentiality of information impact upon Federal information activities."³⁶ The panel was cochaired by Representative Frank Horton (R-NY) and Senator Thomas J. McIntyre (D-NH); conducted its work largely in parallel with the Privacy Protection Study Commission; and produced 36 topical reports, with recommendations, as well as a final summary report of October 3, 1977.³⁷ One of these reports was devoted to confidentiality and privacy. Issued July 29, 1977, it offered 12 recommendations.³⁸ Although a House subcommittee devoted a hearing to the report, no immediate action was taken on its recommendations.³⁹

Subsequently, however, a recommended new organization to centralize and coordinate existing information management functions within the executive branch, and proposed limits on the use of statistical information or disclosing it in identifiable form without the consent of the data subject, were realized in the Paperwork Reduction Act of 1980.⁴⁰ The statute established a new Office of Information and Regulatory Affairs within the Office of Management and Budget (OMB) to assist the OMB director with

---

[35] See U.S. General Services Administration, National Archives and Records Service, Office of the Federal Register, *Public Papers of the Presidents of the United States~ Jimmy Carter, 1979* (Washington: GPO, 1980), pp. 581-587.
[36] 88 Stat. 1789.
[37] U.S. Commission on Federal Paperwork, Final Summary Report: A Report of the Commission on Federal Paperwork (Washington: GPO, 1977).
[38] U.S. Commission on Federal Paperwork, *Confidentiality and Privacy: A Report of the Commission on Federal Paperwork* (Washington: GPO, 1977), pp. 13 9-175.
[39] U.S. Congress. House Committee on Government Operations, Privacy and Confidentiality Report and Final Recommendations of the Commission on Federal Paperwork, hearing, 95th Cong., 1st sess., Oct. 17, 1977 (Washington: GPO, 1978).

the government-wide information coordination and guidance functions assigned to him by the act. Examples of these functions include the OMB director's broad responsibilities for statistical policy and coordination, such as:

> (1) developing long range plans for the improved performance of Federal statistical activities and programs; (2) coordinating, through the review of budget proposals and as otherwise provided in this [statute], the functions of the Federal Government with respect to gathering, interpreting, and disseminating statistics and statistical information; (3) developing and implementing Government-wide policies, principles, standards, and guidelines concerning statistical collection procedures and methods, statistical data classifications, and statistical information presentation and dissemination; and (4) evaluating statistical program performance and agency compliance with Government-wide policies, principles, standards, and guidelines.[41]

Indicating that one of the purposes of the Paperwork Reduction Act was "to ensure that the collection, maintenance, use and dissemination of information by the Federal Government is consistent with applicable laws relating to confidentiality, including the Privacy Act,"[42] the statute assigned the OMB director the following privacy functions: "(1) developing and implementing policies, principles, standards, and guidelines on information disclosure and confidentiality, and on safeguarding the security of information collected or maintained by or on behalf of agencies; (2) providing agencies with advice and guidance about information security, restriction, exchange, and disclosure; and (3) monitoring compliance with [the Privacy Act] and related information management laws."[43] These privacy functions would be expanded, and privacy responsibilities would be specified for the federal agencies, in a 1995 recodification of the act.[44] In 1988, amendments governing computer matches of personal information by government agencies, discussed below, were enacted.[45]

---

[40] 94 Stat. 2812; 44 U.S.C. 3501 *et seq.*
[41] 94 Stat. 2816.
[42] 94 Stat. 2813.
[43] 94 Stat. 2816.
[44] 109 Stat. 163; 44 U.S.C. 3501 *et seq.*
[45] 102 Stat. 2507.

## Family Educational Rights and Privacy Act

Another privacy statute enacted by the 93$^{rd}$ Congress in 1974 was the Family Educational Rights and Privacy Act (FERPA), also known as the Buckley Amendment in reference to its sponsor, Senator James L. Buckley (C/R-NY), who offered the proposal as a floor amendment to the General Education Provisions Act during Senate consideration of the Education Amendments of 1974.[46] As originally approved, the FERPA provided the parents of minor children and students over 18 years of age, the right to inspect, correct, amend, and control the disclosure of information in the education records of educational agencies or institutions receiving federal funds. It also obliged these institutions to inform parents and students of their rights, and to establish policies and procedures for the exercise of such rights.

In its 1977 final report, the Privacy Protection Study Commission assessed the provisions and implementation of the FERPA, and offered several recommendations for clarifying and strengthening the statute.[47] Prior to 1994, Congress amended the FERPA with technical modifications on a few occasions; substantive amendments were effected, primarily, with the Improving America's Schools Act of 1994[48] and, less so, with the Higher Education Amendments of 1998.[49] These included provisions explicitly prohibiting the allocation of federal funds to any state educational agency or institution "that has a policy of denying, or effectively prevents, the parents of students the right to inspect and review the education records maintained by the State ... on their children"; permitting access to student records by "State and local officials or authorities to whom such information is specifically allowed to be reported or disclosed pursuant to State statute ... if the allowed reporting or disclosure concerns the juvenile justice system"; permitting the disclosure of student records to "the entity or person designated in a Federal grand jury subpoena" or in other subpoenas issued "for a law enforcement purpose"; prohibiting an educational agency or institution from releasing students records, "for a period of not less than five years," to a third party that violated the FERPA requirements governing access to such records; and clarifying that nothing in the FERPA prohibits an educational agency or institution from placing relevant disciplinary

---

[46] 88 Stat. 571; 20 U.S.C. 1232g.
[47] U.S. Privacy Protection Study Commission, *Personal Privacy in an Information Society*, pp. 393-444.
[48] 108 Stat. 3924.
[49] 112 Stat. 1835.

information in a student's records or revealing that information to teachers or other school officials "who have legitimate educational interests in the behavior of the student." According to one estimate, "these amendments [were] apparently intended to expand the coverage of FERPA, strengthen incentives to comply with the Act, eliminate schools' and institutions' dilemmas about restricting access to records that are subpoenaed, and prevent the Act from interfering with educational professionals' need to know about students' behavior."[50]

## Financial Privacy Act

As noted above, the Right to Financial Privacy Act of 1978 (RFPA) grew out of the concerns of the Privacy Protection Study Commission for limiting government access to personal records held by a private sector recordkeeper through adherence to recognized legal processes. It was a product of the joint efforts of the Carter Administration and the 95th Congress. The commission's concerns and the cooperative legislative efforts of the two branches to enact the RFPA, as the following contemporaneous comments reflect, were fueled by several recent developments.

> Prior to 1970, there was little need for concern about the privacy of financial records. Bank records were considered confidential by bank officials and records were kept only for internal bank use. This practice was challenged upon the passage of the Bank Secrecy Act of 1970 [84 Stat. 1114]. This legislation was designed to aid government agencies in their investigations of criminal, tax, and regulatory matters. The Bank Secrecy Act requires, *inter alia,* depository institutions to maintain duplicate records of almost all customer transactions. In particular, it requires that checks and other charges in excess of $100 be microfilmed and retained for five years. Banks have found, however, that sorting checks over $99 is so expensive that it is easier and cheaper to microfilm all checks. Concomitant with this development has been an increase in personal checking accounts and an expansion of commercial banking into the open-end credit market. Commercial banks, by complying with the recordkeeping requirements of the Bank Secrecy Act, now possess information about the activities and relationships of millions of people. As a result, the amount of financial and

---

[50] U.S. Library of Congress, Congressional Research Service, *Family Educational Rig/its and Privacy Act: P.L. 103-382 Amendments.* by Richard N. Apling, CRS Report 94-980 EPW (Washington: Dec. 7, 1994), p. 2.

personal information available to the government has been commensurately expanded.

Improved technology has exacerbated this threat to financial privacy. For example, the use of Electronic Funds Transfer services (EFT) promises to increase the amount of personal information available to financial institutions. These services involve the processing and documentation of deposits, withdrawals, and transfers of money with the help of computers and telecommunications. One type of EFT services, point-of-sale services, allows an individual to use finds on deposit without having to visit the financial institution and without having to write a check. The development of point-of-sale services will have several ramifications. First, the expansion of this service will result in an increase in the amount and detail of personal information recorded by financial institutions as it is likely that accounting and administrative information will accompany periodic payment. Second, financial records will become more centralized and accessible. Third, financial records will contain information not usually considered payment data, such as information concerning the purpose of the transaction.

These developments served to increase public concern over privacy during the 1970s. In addition, the Watergate investigations focused attention on privacy interests by disclosing that government officials used information from private financial records to conduct illegitimate investigations of certain individuals.[51]

Then, amidst this atmosphere and the deliberations of the Privacy Protection Study Commission, the Supreme Court's April 21, 1976, decision in *United States* v. *Miller* burst.[52] The respondent, Mitchell Miller, had been convicted of possessing an unregistered still, engaging in the business of a distiller without giving bond and with the intent to defraud the government of whiskey tax, possessing 175 gallons of whiskey for which no taxes had been paid, and conspiring to defraud the United States of tax revenues. Prior to his trial, Miller had moved to suppress copies of checks and other bank records obtained by means of allegedly defective subpoenas *duces tecum* issued by the United States Attorney, not a court, and served on two banks where he had accounts. The banks had maintained the records in compliance with the requirements of the Bank Secrecy Act. The trial court overruled the motion to suppress, and the evidence was admitted. The United States Court

---

[51] Lorena Kern Davitt, "The Right to Financial Privacy Act: New Protection for Financial Records," *Fordham Urban Law Journal,* vol. 8, 1979-1980, pp. 597-599.
[52] *United States* v. *Miller, 425* U.S. 435 (1976).

of Appeals for the Fifth Circuit reversed the decision on the ground that a depositor's Fourth Amendment rights are violated when bank records, maintained pursuant to the Bank Secrecy Act, are obtained by means of a defective subpoena, and held that any evidence so obtained must be suppressed. However, the court rejected Miller's contention that the provisions of the Bank Secrecy Act requiring banks to microfilm all checks violated a depositor's Fourth Amendment right to be free from unreasonable searches and seizures.[53]

Affirmance of the appellate court's ruling seemingly would have established a constitutional right to financial privacy under the Fourth Amendment. However, the Supreme Court, in its 7-2 decision, held:

- The subpoenaed materials were business records of the banks, not respondent's private papers.
- There is no legitimate "expectation of privacy" in the contents of the original checks and deposit slips, since the checks are not confidential communications but negotiable instruments to be used in commercial transactions, and all the documents obtained contain only information voluntarily conveyed to the banks and exposed to their employees in the ordinary course of business. The Fourth Amendment does not prohibit the obtaining of information revealed to a third party and conveyed by him to Government authorities. The [Bank Secrecy] Act record-keeping requirements do not alter these considerations so as to create a protectable Fourth Amendment interest of a bank depositor in the bank's records of his account.
- Issuance of a subpoena to a third party does not violate a defendant's rights, even if a criminal prosecution is contemplated at the time the subpoena is issued.
- Access to bank records under the [Bank Secrecy] Act is to be controlled by "existing legal process." That does not mean that greater judicial scrutiny, equivalent to that required for a search warrant, is necessary when a subpoena is used to obtain a depositor's bank records.[54]

---

[53] 500 F.2d 751 (5th Cir. 1974).
[54] 425 U.S. 435-436.

In brief, the *Miller* decision effectively gave the federal government unrestricted access to a bank customer's or depositor's financial records through administrative subpoena. The Privacy Protection Study Commission disagreed with the breadth of the *Miller* decision and proffered corrective recommendations.[55] From these origins came the Right to Financial Privacy Act (RFPA). Enacted as Title XI of the far-ranging Financial Institutions Regulatory and Interest Rate Control Act of 1978, the RFPA prohibits any federal agency from obtaining access to financial records of the customers of a financial institution, except when access is required in connection with a legitimate law enforcement inquiry, unless one of five specified procedures is followed: (1) customer authorization; (2) administrative summons or subpoena, which is authorized by law, judicially enforceable, used in connection with a legitimate law enforcement inquiry, and with advance notice to the customer; (3) search warrant, which meets the existing "probable cause" standard for the issuance of such instruments and with advance notice to the customer; (4) judicial subpoena; or *(5)* formal written request, which is designed for federal agencies which do not have administrative summons or subpoena authority.[56]

The concept of "financial institutions" is broadly defined to include all banking-type and consumer finance businesses, as well as credit unions and companies issuing credit cards, located within the United States or its territories. The term "customer" is narrowly defined to include only natural persons or partnerships of five or fewer individuals who utilize a financial institution in connection with an account maintained under the individual's or partnership's name. "Financial records" is broadly defined to mean "an original copy of, a copy of, or information known to have been derived from, any record held by a financial institution pertaining to a customer's relationship with the financial institution."

The RFPA provides procedures which a customer may follow to challenge an attempt by a government agency to obtain access to his or her financial records under the terms of the statute. A civil penalties provision prescribes damage awards to customers when federal agencies or financial institutions are found to be obtaining or disclosing financial records or information in violation of the RFPA.

---

[55] See US. Privacy Protection Study Commission, *Personal Privacy in an Information Society,* pp. *362-373.*
[56] 92 Stat. 3697; 12 U.S.C. 3401 *et seq.*

## Privacy Protection Act

Congress enacted the Privacy Protection Act of 1980 to protect a First Amendment right of privacy threatened by police searches. The statute was prompted by a Supreme Court ruling involving a Stanford University newspaper complaint. On April 12, 1971, four local police officers, armed with a search warrant, conducted a Do-notice, surprise search of the offices of the *Stanford Daily,* a student newspaper published at Stanford University. They were seeking unpublished photographs which they believed would assist them in identifying the assailants of fellow officers injured at a recent demonstration before the Stanford University Hospital The officers, after thoroughly exploring the newspaper offices, failed to find the photographs. Subsequently, both they and the local district attorney were sued, pursuant to 42 U.S.C. 1983, by staff members of the student newspaper alleging violations of their civil rights and contending that a subpoena, rather than a search warrant, should have been used. Both the federal trial and appellate courts agreed with the plaintiffs that the Fourth and Fourteenth Amendments barred issuing warrants to search for materials held by nonsuspect third parties when no probable cause was shown that a subpoena, which can be challenged in court before being enforced, would be impractical. On May 31, 1978, the Supreme Court, in a 5-3 decision, ruled that the Constitution did not bar police officers from obtaining warrants and then making unannounced searches of newspaper offices for evidence, even though neither the newspaper nor its reporters were suspected of criminal activity.[57]

Sorting out the ramifications of the court's decision, Congress responded with the Privacy Protection Act of 1980, which prohibits federal, state, and local law enforcement officers from using warrants to search and seize "work products" of news and other organizations engaged in First Amendment activities, except in specified circumstances; defines "work products" as materials prepared for communicating information to the public, including mental impressions, conclusions, opinions, or theories of the person who prepared the material; prohibits federal, state, and local law enforcement officers from seizing "documentary materials" from persons engaged in First Amendment activities, except in specified circumstances; defines "documentary materials" as materials upon which information is recorded, including written or printed materials, photographs, films, negatives, and video and audio tapes; provides a civil cause of action for

---

[57] *Zurcher v. Stanford Daily,* 436 U.S. 547(1978).

damages for any person aggrieved by a search for, or seizure of, materials in violation of the statute; requires the Attorney General to issue guidelines for the procedures to be employed by federal officers in searching for evidence held by a person not suspected of a crime; and allows administrative Sanctions against any Department of Justice officer or employee who violates such guidelines, but prohibits a private individual from filing a lawsuit regarding such a violation.[58]

## Cable Communications Policy Act

The day before its final adjournment, the 98th Congress approved the Cable Communications Policy Act of 1984, culminating a four-year effort to balance the rights of the industry against those of the cities that granted franchises.[59] Section 631 of the statute requires cable services to provide subscribers an initial and, thereafter, an annual, written statement concerning the services' collection, use, and management of personally identifiable information with respect to subscribers. Information required to be included in this statement is specified in the section. A cable subscriber has a right of access to all personally identifiable information regarding himself or herself which is collected and maintained by a cable service, and may correct any error in such information. A cable service may use the cable system to collect personally identifiable information in order to obtain information necessary to render a cable or other service provided by the cable operator to the subscriber or to detect unauthorized reception of cable communications. With very limited exceptions, a cable service is prohibited from disclosing personally identifiable information concerning any subscriber without his or her prior consent. Any person aggrieved by any act of a cable service in violation of Section 631 may bring a civil action and the court may award actual damages, punitive damages, and litigation costs and attorney fees reasonably incurred.

## Electronic Communications Privacy Act

In October 1986, Congress cleared legislation providing privacy protection to communications transmitted with new forms of technology.

---

[58] 94 Stat. 1879; 42 U.S.C. 2000aa *et seq.*
[59] 98 Stat. 2779.

The Electronic Communications Privacy Act of 1986 (ECPA) extends existing privacy guarantees for conventional telephones to cellular telephones operated by high-frequency radio waves, transmissions by private satellite, paging devices, and electronic mail messages transmitted by, and stored in, computers.[60]

Title I of the statute amends the federal criminal code to extend the prohibition against the unauthorized interception of wire and oral communications to include, with some exceptions, specific types of electronic communications and the communications of any provider of wire or electronic communication services. Providers of an electronic communication service, with specified exceptions, are prohibited from knowingly divulging the contents of any communication carried on that service. Any person whose wire, oral, or electronic communication is intercepted, disclosed, or intentionally used in violation of chapter 119 of the federal criminal code may bring a civil action to recover damages, but must do so not later than two years after the date upon which the alleged violation was discovered. The title also specifies additional crimes for which the interception of wire, oral, or electronic communication can be authorized in order to facilitate the investigation of such crimes. It provides additional requirements for applications, court orders, and the implementation of court orders for the interception of such communications. Certain intelligence activities approved by the Attorney General are not to be affected by the communications interception provisions of chapters 119 and 121 of the federal criminal code, and allowance is made for a court-authorized mobile tracking device to be used outside the jurisdiction of the authorizing court. The warning of a person that he or she is the subject of electronic surveillance is made a criminal offense, and a final provision allows the Attorney General to initiate a civil action to obtain an injunction to prevent felony level violations of the ECPA.

Title II, concerning stored wire and electronic communications and transactional records access, makes it a criminal offense to access, without authorization, a facility through which an electronic communication service is provided, or to exceed an authorized access to such a facility. It also prohibits the provider of an electronic communication service or remote computing service, except under certain circumstances, from divulging the contents of any communication stored, carried, or maintained by such service. The title specifies procedural requirements for a government entity

---

[60] 100 Stat. 1848.

to obtain access to electronic communications in electronic storage, including court-ordered creation of back-up copies of the contents of such communications. Provision is made for any subscriber or customer of a communication service who is aggrieved by a willful or intentional violation the title, which is chapter 121 of the federal criminal code, to initiate a civil action to recover appropriate relief. Lastly, the director of the Federal Bureau of Investigation (FBI) is granted access to telephone or communication service information and records relevant to any authorized foreign counterintelligence investigation. No officer, employee, or agent of a wire or electronic communication service provider may disclose to any person that the FBI has sought or obtained such access to telephone or communication service information.

Title III of the statute addresses the use of pen registers and trap and trace devices. A pen register is a device that records or decodes numbers dialed or otherwise transmitted by telephone; a trap and trace device captures an incoming electronic or other impulse and can identify the number from which the call was made. The title prohibits the installation or use of a pen register or a trap and trace device without a court order pursuant to the ECPA or the Foreign Intelligence Surveillance Act of 1978, and imposes criminal penalties for violations of this prohibition.[61] Government attorneys and state law enforcement officers are authorized to apply for a court order allowing the installation and use of a pen register or a trap and trace device, a certification by the applicant that information likely to be obtained by such an installation is relevant to an ongoing criminal investigation being required for the issuance of such an order. Furthermore, providers of a wire or electronic communication service, landlords, custodians, and other persons are required to furnish all information, facilities, and technical assistance necessary to accomplish the ill stallation of a pen register or a trap and trace device if such assistance is ordered by the court. Anyone so providing such assistance shall be compensated for any reasonable expenses incurred, and no cause of action shall lie in any Court against anyone so providing such assistance. The Attorney General must report annually to Congress on the number of applications made by law enforcement agencies of the Department of Justice for pen register and trap and trace device orders.

---

[61] The latter statute may be found at 50 U.S.C. 1801 *et seq.*

## Computer Security Act

Recognizing the increasing use of computers by federal agencies and the vulnerability of computer-stored information, including personal information, to unauthorized access, Congress enacted the Computer Security Act of 1987.[62] The statute requires each federal agency to develop security plans for its computer systems containing sensitive information. Such plans are subject to review by the National Institute of Standards and Technology (NIST) of the Department of Commerce and a summary, together with overall budget plans for information technology, is fled with OMIB. NIST is authorized to set security standards for all federal computer systems except those containing intelligence, cryptologic, or certain military information, or information specifically authorized under criteria established by an executive order or statute to be kept secret in the interest of national defense or foreign policy. The statute also mandates a Computer Systems Security and Privacy Advisory Board within the Department of Commerce, which, among other duties, is to identify emerging managerial, technical, administrative, and physical safeguard issues relative to computer systems security and privacy and advise NIST and the Secretary of Commerce on security and privacy issues pertaining to federal computer systems. Each federal agency is directed to provide all employees involved with the management, use, or operation of its computer systems with mandatory periodic training in computer security awareness and accepted computer security practice.

## Computer Matching and Privacy Protection Act

Congress amended the Privacy Act in 1988 to regulate the use of computer matching conducted by federal agencies or making use of federal records subject to the statute. The amendments were denominated the Computer Matching and Privacy Protection Act of 1988.[63] A controversial matter for more than 10 years, computer matching—the computerized comparison of records for the purpose of establishing or verifying eligibility for a federal benefit program or for recouping payments or delinquent debts under such programs—had begun in 1977 at the Department of Health and

---

[62] 101 Stat. 1724.
[63] 102 Stat. 2507.

Human Services. The effort, dubbed Project Match, compared welfare rolls in selected jurisdictions with federal payroll records in the same areas. The controversy surrounding this and similar computerized matches pitted privacy protection advocates, who alleged that personally identifiable data were being used for purposes other than those prompting their collection, against those using the technique to ferret out fraud, abuse, and the overpayment of federal benefits. As the practice subsequently became more widespread, controversy over its use grew.

The amendments regulate the use of computer matching by federal agencies involving personally identifiable records maintained in a system of records subject to the Privacy Act. Matches performed for statistical, research, law enforcement, tax, and certain other purposes are not subject to such regulation. In order for matches to occur, a written matching agreement, effectively creating a matching program, must be prepared specifying such details, as explicitly required by the amendments, as the purpose and Legal authority for the program; the justification for the program and the anticipated results, including a specific estimate of any savings; a description of the records being matched; procedures for providing individualized notice, at the time of application, to applicants for and recipients of financial assistance or payments under federal benefits programs and to applicants for and holders of positions as federal personnel that any information they provide may be subject to verification through the matching program; procedures for verifying information produced in the matching program; and procedures for the retention, security, and timely destruction of the records matched and for the security of the results of the matching program. Copies of such matching agreements are transmitted to congressional oversight committees and are available to the public upon request. Executive oversight of, and guidance for, matching programs is vested in the director of OMB. Notice of the establishment or revision of a matching program must be published in the *Federal Register* 30 days in advance of implementation.

The amendments also require every agency conducting or participating in a matching program to establish a "Data Integrity Board," composed of senior agency officials, to oversee and coordinate program operations, including the execution of certain specified review, approval, and reporting responsibilities.

Agencies are prohibited from reducing, suspending, or terminating financial assistance to an individual without first verifying the accuracy of computerized data used in the matching program and without first giving the individual 30 days to contest the action.

## Video Privacy Protection Act

Another 1988 privacy statute was enacted in response to an incident that occurred during the 1987 fight over the unsuccessful nomination of Robert H. Bork to the Supreme Court. During the Bork confirmation hearings, a reporter obtained and published a list of the videotapes the Bork family had rented, prompting an outcry from members of Congress in both political parties who felt Bork's privacy had been invaded. A legislative response was enacted the following year. The Video Privacy Protection Act of 1988 prohibits videotape service providers from disclosing their customers' names, addresses, and specific videotapes rented or purchased, except in specifically defined circumstances.[64] Such exceptions include disclosure to the customer; to any person with the informed, written Consent of the customer given at the time the disclosure was sought; to a law enforcement agency pursuant to a warrant, grand jury subpoena, or court order; or, name and address only, to a direct marketing business, as Long as the customer has an opportunity to reject such a disclosure. Any person aggrieved by any action of a person in violation of the statute may bring a civil action, the court being authorized to award actual damages, punitive damages, and litigation costs and attorneys fees reasonably incurred. Such a lawsuit must be initiated within two years of the discovery of the alleged violation.

## Driver's Privacy Protection Act

Enacted as Title XXX of the omnibus Violent Crime Control and Law Enforcement Act of 1994, the Driver's Privacy Protection Act (DPPA) prohibits a state department of motor vehicles, and any officer, employee, or contractor of such an entity, from knowingly disclosing or otherwise making available to any person "personal information about any individual obtained by the department in connection with a motor vehicle record" without the driver's consent.[65] Explicit exceptions to this rule include "matters of motor vehicle or driver safety and theft, motor vehicle emissions, motor vehicle product alterations, recalls, or advisories, performance monitoring of motor vehicles and dealers by motor vehicle manufacturers, and removal of non-owner records from the original owner records of motor vehicle

---

[64] 102 Stat. 3195; 18 U.S.C. 2710 note.
[65] 108 Stat. 2099; 18 U.S.C. 2721 note.

manufacturers to carry out the purposes" of certain enumerated statutes. A criminal fine may be levied against any person who knowingly violates the statute, and a civil penalty of not more than $5,000 may be imposed by the Attorney General against a state department of motor vehicles for each day of substantial noncompliance. A civil action may be brought against a person who knowingly violates the DPPA by the driver whose privacy was compromised by the violation.

On January 12, 2000, the Supreme Court unanimously ruled that the DPPA is a valid exercise of the constitutional authority of Congress to regulate commerce, and does not violate the 10$^{th}$ Amendment.[66] The drivers' information that the statute governs was seen as being used by insurers, marketers, and others engaged in interstate commerce to contact drivers with customized solicitations, making this information "an article of commerce" subject to congressional regulation. Relying on a 1988 ruling, the court found the DPPA does not "commandeer" states into enforcing federal law applicable to private entities.[67] The statute regulates state activities directly rather than seeking to control the manner in which states regulate private parties. Also, the DPPA was seen as generally applicable, regulating both the states as initial suppliers and private parties that resell drivers' information—"the universe of entities that participate as suppliers to the market for motor vehicles."

## Telecommunications Act

Enacted in response to significant structure and marketing changes occurring within the telecommunications industry, the Telecommunications Act of 1996 is a major rewrite of national telecommunications policy, establishing a single, comprehensive regulatory framework that will capture the benefits of competition while ensuring that the users and suppliers of a developing and diversified information industry will be protected from exploitative practices and abuse).[68] Among the provisions of the statute, section 702 specifies that, except as required by law or with the approval of the customer, a telecommunications carrier receiving or obtaining customer proprietary network information by virtue of its provision of a telecommunications service shall only use, disclose, or permit access to

---

[66] *Reno v. Condon*, 120 S.Ct. 666; 68 USLW 4037 (Jan. 12, 2000).
[67] See South Carolina v. Baker, 485 U.S. 505 (1988).
[68] 110 Stat. 56.

individually identifiable customer proprietary network information in providing the telecommunications service from which such information derives or services necessary to, or used in, the provision of such telecommunications service, including the publishing of directories. Upon affirmative written request of the customer, a telecommunications carrier shall disclose that customer's proprietary network information to any person designated by the customer, including the customer himself or herself. Customer proprietary network information, according to the statute, is information that relates to the quantity, technical configuration, type, destination, and amount of use of a telecommunications service subscribed to by any customer of a telecommunications carrier, and that is made available to the carrier by the customer solely by virtue of the carrier-customer relationship, and includes, as well, information contained in the bills pertaining to telephone exchange service or telephone toll service received by a customer of a carrier, but does not include subscriber list information.

## Health Insurance Portability and Accountability Act

Compared with the Clinton Administration's famous, but failed, 1994 plan to overhaul the entire health care system, the Health Insurance Portability and Accountability Act of 1996 (HIPAA) was miniature in scope.[69] The statute sought to guarantee the portability of health insurance coverage for individuals who had health insurance benefits. It also created a pilot program for medical savings accounts, increased the deductibility of health insurance for the self-employed, and provided tax breaks to increase the use of long-term care insurance.

Of particular interest for privacy protection are provisions of the statute's administrative simplification instructing the Secretary of Health and Human Services (HHS) to develop standards to support electronic data interchange for a variety of administrative and financial health care transactions. Specifically, HIPAA requires the Secretary to issue regulations to establish standard electronic formats for billing and other common transactions, including the use of uniform data codes for reporting diagnoses, referrals, authorizations, and medical procedures; mandates the development of unique identifiers *(i.e.,* identification numbers) for patients, employers,

---

[69] 110 Stat. 1936.

health plans, and health care providers; and requires the Secretary to issue security standards, including an electronic signature standard, to safeguard confidential health information against unauthorized access, disclosure, and misuse.

Beyond these obligations, the subtitle prescribes a timetable for Congress and the Secretary to develop comprehensive medical records privacy standards which would define the circumstances under which the uses and disclosures of such information required a patient's authorization, and gave patients the right to access and amend their personally identifiable health information. The Secretary was required to report to Congress by August 1997 on ways to protect the privacy of personally identifiable health information; Congress was given two years after receiving that report to enact health records privacy legislation, and, if it failed to do so, the Secretary was instructed to issue health privacy regulations by February 21, 2000.[70] As discussed below, the Secretary presented her recommendations to Congress on September 11, 1997, and, because Congress did not enact legislation guided by those recommendations, she issued proposed health records privacy regulations on November 3, 1999.

## Children's Online Privacy Protection Act

Although the Clinton Administration and many members of Congress preferred to rely upon industry self regulation for realizing Internet privacy protection, frustration with the industry's slow response regarding minors led to the enactment of the Children's Online Privacy Protection Act of 1998 (COPPA) as part of the Omnibus Consolidated and Emergency Supplemental Appropriations Act, 1999.[71] The statute requires the operator of a commercial Web site or online service targeted at children under the age of 13 to provide clear notice of information collection and use practices; to obtain verifiable parental consent prior to collecting, using, and disseminating personal information about children under 13; and to provide parents access to their children's personal information and the option to prevent its further use. On October 20, 1999, the Federal Trade Commission issued a final rule to implement the COPPA.[72] The statute authorizes the

---

[70] 110 Stat. 2021; 42 U.S.C. 1320d.
[71] 112 Stat. 2681-728; 15 U.S.C. 6501-6506.
[72] *Federal Register,* vol. 64, Nov. 3, 1999, pp. 59888-59915.

commission to bring enforcement actions and impose civil penalties for violations of the rule in the same manner as for its other rules.

## Gramm-Leach-Bliley Act

Enacted in November 1999, the Gramm-Leach-Bliley Act constitutes a historic overhaul of federal laws governing the financial services industry.[73] Repealing laws restricting cross-ownership among banks, brokerages, and insurers, the statute establishes a new regulatory framework for maintaining the safety and stability of the financial services industry and requires a number of regulatory agencies to develop new regulations for its implementation. Named for its principal congressional champions—Senator Phil Gramm (R-TX), Representative James A. Leach (R-VA), and Representative Tom Bliley (R-VA)—the statute requires relevant federal regulatory agencies to issue rules obligating financial institutions to establish standards to insure the security and confidentiality of customer records; prohibits financial institutions from disclosing nonpublic personal information to unaffiliated third parties without providing customers the opportunity to decline such disclosures; prohibits financial institutions from disclosing customer account numbers to unaffiliated third parties for use in telemarketing, direct mail marketing, and e-mail marketing; requires financial institutions to disclose, when a customer relationship is initially established and annually thereafter, their privacy policies, including their polices regarding the sharing of information with affiliates and unaffiliated third parties; and mandates a study of the information sharing practices among financial institutions and their affiliates to be conducted by the Secretary of the Treasury, relevant regulatory agencies, and the Federal Trade Commission. Regulatory agency rules implementing these privacy protections are to be promulgated within six months after the enactment of the statute and are to become effective on November 12, 2000.

## Safe Harbor Privacy Principles

On July 21, 2000, the Department of Commerce issued a set of Safe Harbor Privacy Principles to enable U.S. companies receiving personal data transfers from European Union (EU) countries to meet the "adequacy" requirements of the EU's *Directive on the Protection of Individuals with Regard to the Processing of Personal Data and the Free Movement of Such Data.* [74] This directive requires all 15 EU member states to make their national privacy laws consistent with the directive, and permits the EU to limit the flow of data among Countries not having corn parable protections for personally identifiable data. The U.S. approach to privacy, which differs from that of the European Community, relies upon a sectoral approach, based upon a combination of legislation, regulation, and self-regulation. Because of these differences in approach, U.S. companies feared that the EU directive might impede the flow of information from EU states if the United States were deemed to have inadequate privacy protection in critical areas such as medical information.

To address this concern, the Commerce Department, through negotiations with the European Commission, and in consultation with U.S. industry and the general public, developed the Safe Harbor Privacy Principles to ensure that data flows between the EU and the United States are not interrupted. Organizations receiving personal data transfers from the EU and complying with the principles should be considered to meet the "adequacy" requirements of the directive. The European Commission is expected to issue an "adequacy determination" for the safe harbor arrangement soon.[75]

# PRIVACY ISSUES BEFORE CONGRESS

## Comprehensive Review

During the 20$^{th}$ century, comprehensive reviews of personal privacy issues were undertaken by the Privacy Protection Study Commission and, to a lesser extent, the Commission on Federal Paperwork, both panels reporting in 1977. These commissions recommended the creation of a permanent federal agency to address, exclusively or in balanced measure, personal privacy matters. Some realization of this proposal occurred with the establishment of the Office of Information and Regulatory Affairs within

---

[73] 113 Stat. 1338.
[74] See *Federal Register*, vol. 65, July 24, 2000, pp. 45665-45686.
[75] For information concerning further developments regarding the Safe Harbor Principles, see the Department of Commerce Web site at

OMB, which, critics allege, has shown only limited interest in privacy since its creation in 1980.[76]

In a climate of opinion supportive of government downsizing, the creation of a new federal privacy review agency is considered not likely to occur. Indeed, the chartering of such an entity has not been legislatively proposed in Congress for almost a decade.[77]

Alternatively, an existing agency might be tasked with performing studies and evaluations that would collectively result in a comprehensive review of personal privacy issues. This approach, however, presents problems of finding a host agency having a sufficiently broad and compatible mandate to support the desired studies and evaluations; assuring that the host agency has adequate resources to perform the desired studies and evaluations; and assuring that the host agency would not relegate its new privacy responsibilities to a low level of priority.

Another, perhaps less encumbered, alternative would be a temporary privacy study body. Producing a comprehensive review of personal privacy issues would be the only mission of the entity, and all of its resources would be devoted to that mission. The operating arrangements and products of the Privacy Protection Study Commission provide precedential models for a new entity, and the resulting final report might offer findings and recommendations that could have currency for a few years, allowing the development of implementing proposals and related legislative strategies conducive with the agendas of relevant congressional committees of jurisdiction.

In the 106$^{th}$ Congress, three bills were introduced to establish a temporary study commission to examine personal privacy issues. One of these, offered in the House on March 21, 2000, by Representative Asa Hutchinson (R-AR) as the Privacy Commission Act (H.R. 4049), would have created a 17-member Commission for the Comprehensive Study of Privacy Protection to "conduct a study of issues relating to protection of individual privacy and the appropriate balance to be achieved between protecting individual privacy and allowing appropriate uses of information."

---

[http://www.ita.doc.gov/tdlecom/menu.html].

[76] See Robert M. Gellman, "Fragmented, Incomplete, and Discontinuous: The Failure of Federal Privacy Regulatory Proposals and Institutions," *Software Law Journal,* vol. 6, April 1993, pp. 199-238.

[77] See, however, Robert Gellman, "Taming the Privacy Monster: A Proposal for a Non-Regulatory Privacy Agency," *Government Information Quarterly,* vol. 17, no. 3, 2000, pp. 235-241.

The final report of the panel would have been submitted to the President and Congress not later than 18 months after the appointment of all of the members of the commission. Referred to the Committee on Government Reform, the bill was considered at a May 16, 2000, hearing before the Subcommittee on Government Management, Information, and Technology. At this hearing, OIRA Administrator John I. Spotila expressed the concern of the Clinton Administration "that some might use the commission as a reason to delay much-needed privacy legislation." Another witness, Minnesota Attorney General Mike Hatch, offered similar views, saying "further study is not the proper course, given the volume of ink already spilled on the privacy subject as well as the volume of consumer outcry and violations." He contended that the commission could delay enforcement and legislative action at the federal and state levels; that it would discover "what everyone already knows: that companies collect a lot of information and disclose it without our knowledge"; and that constituents want, not a privacy study, but real privacy protection now.

Supporting the legislation, Robert R. Belair, former deputy counsel of the presidential Committee on the Right of Privacy during the Ford Administration and Office of Telecommunication Policy attorney responsible for Carter Administration follow-up projects based the Privacy Protection Study Commission recommendations, thought "the work of the privacy commission will lead to better decisions about privacy." Joining him in supporting the bill, Georgetown University professor of electronic commerce Mary J. Culnan cautioned that the commission' "usefulness will be short-lived if it only focuses on today' technologies and privacy issues and fails to address ... emerging issues."[78]

Amidst such divided opinion, the Subcommittee on Government Management amended the bill on June 14, increasing the panel's funding authorization from $2.5 million to $5 million; authorizing it to issue subpoenas to obtain needed information, but prohibiting the panel from acquiring any classified information relating to national security; and reducing the number of required field hearings from 20 to 10. Forwarded to the full Committee on Government Reform, the bill was further amended on June 29 before being ordered to be reported, as modified, to the House. One amendment indicated that prompt passage of privacy protections could occur before the commission competed its work; another tasked the panel with studying financial fraud against elderly people victimized by schemers who

---

[78] Shruti Date, "Privacy Commission Proposal Gets an Unenthusiastic Reception," *Government Computer News*, Vol.19, June 12, 2000, pp. 12, 14.

gain access to their banking and investment records; a third required banks and other financial institutions to seek objective, third-party audits of their computer safeguards to assure depositors and investors that their records are secure; and a final amendment added civil liberties experts to the diverse membership of the panel. Brought up on the floor on October 2, 2000, for approval under a suspension of the House rules, the bill failed to pass on a vote of 250 yeas to 146 nays (two thirds approval required).[79]

## Privacy Act Amendment

Several issues are before the 107th Congress regarding the Privacy Act. As noted earlier, a September 2000 GAO found that 23 of 70 agencies had disclosed personal information gathered from their Web sites to third parties, mostly other agencies, but at least four were discovered to be sharing such information with private entities. Responding to these findings, some privacy advocates called for updating the Privacy Act to specify privacy protections for Internet visitors to executive agency Web sites, while others urged better oversight and enforcement of the statute.[80]

Another issue concerns continued vestment of Privacy Act oversight and enforcement in the director of OMB or, alternatively, in another entity. Options for consideration in this regard include a small privacy agency having no regulatory authority over the private sector[81] or a Chief Information Officer of the United States (CIOUS). A Progressive Policy Institute report recommended such a position in March 2000,[82] and legislation in support of the concept was offered in the House during the

---

[79] *Congressional Record*, daily edition, vol. 146, Oct. 2, 2000, pp. H8561-H8570, H8588-H85 89.

[80] Lance Gay, "GAO Finds Agencies Sharing Data of On-line Visitors," *Washington Times*, Sept. 8, 2000, p. A3; U.S. General Accounting Office, *Internet Privacy: Agencies' Efforts to Implement OMB 's Privacy Policy*, GAO Report GAO/GGD-00-191 (Washington: September 2000).

[81] See Robert Gellman, "Taming the Privacy Monster: A Proposal for a Non-Regulatory Privacy Agency," *Government Information Quarterly*, vol. 17, no. 3, 2000, pp. 235-241.

[82] See Robert D. Atkinson and Jacob Ulevich, *Digital Government: The Next Step to Reengineering the Federal Government* (Washington: Progressive Policy Institute, March 2000), p. 13.

106th Congress.[83] Texas Governor George W. Bush, the anticipated Republican presidential nominee, endorsed the CIOUS idea in a June 9, 2000, government reform speech in Philadelphia. During a September 2000 House subcommittee hearing on the proffered CIOUS bills[84] and in related published views, proponents of the new position contended that many aspects of information technology (IT) management would benefit from having a IT expert in charge of this area, that such an official would better facilitate OMB oversight of IT applications and use, and that efficiencies and economies could well result if this official could prevent federal agencies from purchasing computer systems that did not work or otherwise performed poorly in, or failed, security tests. Critics maintained that the CIOUS would unnecessarily perform a subset of duties currently vested in the OMB deputy director for management, would seemingly have little immediate enforcement powers, and, in some versions, might be controlling funds outside the traditional appropriations process. Members of the CIO Council reportedly are at odds over the need for the CIOUS.[85]

A third issue concerns inclusion of the White House Office and the Office of the Vice President within the scope of the Privacy Act, and to what extent, if any, the legislative branch should be subject to the statute or parallel requirements set by rule or standing order. Disclosures of personally identifiable information by the White House during the Clinton Administration has fueled this issue. Similarly, although Congress and the legislative support agencies are not subject to the Privacy Act, the issue of legislatively requiring such is fueled by considerations of executive and legislative branch parity in this regard, as well as by the deemed need for more explicit privacy protections within the legislative branch.[86]

---

[83] H.R. 4670 was introduced on June 15 by Rep. Jim Turner (D-TX), and H.R. 5024 was introduced on July 27 by Rep. Tom Davis (R-VA); both bills were referred to the Committee on Government Reform.

[84] U.S. Congress, House Committee on Government Reform, Subcommittee on Government Management, Information, and Technology, *Establishing a Federal CIO: Information Technology Management and Assurance Within the Federal Government*, bearing, 106th Cong., 2nd sess., Sept. 12, 2000 (Washington: transcript awaiting publication).

[85] See Christopher J. Dorobek, "Experts Debate Need for Federal IT Czar," *Govern,nent Computer News*, vol. 19, Mar. 6, 2000, p. 58; Christopher I. Dorobek, "CI0 Council on Track, Members Say," *Government Computer News*, vol. 19, May 8, 2000, p. *65;* Christopher I. Dorobek, "What Would Governmentwide CJ0 Do?," *Government Computer News*, vol. 19, July 10, 2000, p. 74; Joseph J. Petrillo, "David Bill Would Give IT Czar Carrots, but No Stick," *Go~ierntnent Cornpwer News*, vol. 19, Sept. 11, 2000, p. 24.

[86] See U.S. Congress, House Committee on Government Reform, Subcommittee on Criminal Justice, Drug Policy, and Human Resources, *The Privacy Act and the*

A fourth issue arises from a September 2000 federal district court ruling that the *Feres* doctrine, which prohibits military personnel from suing the government for injuries, applies equally to lawsuits brought under the Privacy Act, resulting in a prohibition on suing not only for damages, but also even for the correction of records.[87]

Still another issue concerns the possible modification of the "routine use" clause of the Privacy Act to improve citizen awareness of the routine uses that agencies have indicated they will make of personally identifiable information and to limit the discretion of agency officials to share personally identifiable information with other agencies. The Privacy Act requires each agency in possession of systems of records to publish for each system the routine uses to which the information might be put. Such notices are published in the *Federal Register*. Most citizens are unaware of these notices and their implications, with the result that they have little understanding of how information supplied by or about them to government agencies might be used. Furthermore, in the view of one policy analyst examining the situation, "agency officials have interpreted the routine use clause broadly and have created almost unlimited ability to move data among Federal agencies."[88]

Finally, an issue has arisen regarding the circumstances, if any, when computer matching of personally identifiable information in systems of records across government programs and agencies should be permitted. Agency officials responsible for combating waste, fraud, and abuse in federal benefits programs urge a reconsideration of the Privacy Acts strict matching requirements, while privacy advocates would retain the status quo.[89]

## Banking and Financial Transactions

As noted above in the discussion of the recently enacted Gramm-Leach-Bliley Act, this statute requires various regulatory agencies to develop new

---

*Presidency*, hearing, 106$^{th}$ Cong., 2$^{nd}$ sess., Sept. 8, 2000 (Washington: transcript awaiting publication).

[87] *Mary Louise Cummings v. Department of the Navy*, Civil Action No. 98-1183 (D.C. D.C., Sept. 6, 2000).

[88] Gloria Cox, "Implementation of the Routine Use Clause of the Privacy Act," *Policy Studies Review*, vol. 10, Winter 1991-1992, p. 43.

regulations to implement its provisions, including those pertaining to privacy protection. Before the legislation was signed into law, bills had been introduced to modify its privacy provisions, and industry experience with new regulatory rules may prompt other attempts at fine-tuning the statute.[90] So, too, may the findings, conclusions, and recommendations resulting from the mandated study of the information sharing practices among financial institutions and their affiliates to be conducted by the Secretary of the Treasury, relevant regulatory agencies, and the Federal Trade Commission.[91]

Other recent developments coming to congressional attention include the "know your customer" rules proposed by banking regulators which would have required banks to report suspicious transactions to federal officials in an effort to detect money laundering and other crimes.[92] These elicited considerable public opposition as an invasion of personal privacy. Shortly after the comment period ended on March 8, 1999, the regulators withdrew their rulemaking proposals. The Federal Deposit Insurance Corporation reported receiving 254,394 comments, for example, and the Board of Governors of the Federal Reserve indicated receipt of "over 17,000 comments." Of these, both entities noted, the "overwhelming majority ... were strongly opposed to the adoption of the proposed regulation."[93] By this time, several bills had been introduced to block the proposed rules,[94] and a House subcommittee held a hearing to explore the invasion of privacy implications of the regulations.[95] Whether these regulations will be proposed again in some modified form is uncertain.

## Medical Records

Current efforts to legislate privacy protection for medical records are, in many regards, a renewal of the failed 1980 attempt to act upon the

---

[89] See U.S. General Accounting Office, The Challenge of Data Sharing: Results of a GAO-Sponsored Symposium on Benefit and Loan Programs, GAO Report GAO-01-67 (Washington: October 2000).

[90] These bills included H.R. 3320 and S. 1903, and, subsequently, S. 1924.

[91] See U.S. Library of Congress, Congressional Research Service, Banking and Financial Services Briefing Book, CRS Electronic Briefing Book, found at [http://www.congress.gov/brbklhtml/ebfinl.html].

[92] Federal Register, vol. 63, Dec. 7, 1998, pp. 67516-67542.

[93] Ibid., vol. 64, Mar. 29, 1999, p. 14845, and Mar. 31, 1999, p. 15210.

[94] See, for example, H.R. 516, H.R. 530, H.R. 575, H.R. 621, S. 403, S. 466, and S. 508.

[95] U.S. Congress, House Committee on the Judiciary, Subcommittee on Commercial and Administrative Law, "Know Your Customer" Rules: Privacy in the Hands of Federal Regulators, hearing, 106th Cong., I" sess., Mar. 4, 1999 (Washington: GPO, 2000).

recommendations of the Privacy Protection Study Commission. A laboriously crafted compromise on medical records legislation collapsed in the final days of the 98$^{th}$ Congress because sponsors could not reconcile the conflicting demands of civil libertarians, psychiatrists, and the intelligence and law enforcement communities. The proposal basically would have applied the principles of the Code of Fair Information Practice, developed by the HEW Secretary's Advisory Committee on Automated Personal Data Systems in 1973, to the patient records of medical and health institutions, not to those kept by private physicians.

Several developments have prompted the recent return to legislating medical records privacy. Growth in the application of information technologies to all aspects of health care and structural changes in health care delivery and payment systems have not only offered significant opportunities for providing improved health care at contained costs, but also increased the threats to patient privacy and medical records confidentiality. Examples include the use of electronic medical records for maintaining clinical information and the use of telemedicine to provide remote access to physicians, medical equipment, and diagnostic facilities by underserved communities. A 1997 study by the National Research Council reported that "the health care industry spent an estimated $10 billion to $15 billion on information technology in 1996."[96]

Major organizational changes in the health care industry also have provided an impetus for expanding the use of information technology. There is a greater need to integrate information provided by participating institutions that are part of managed care systems, as compared to fee-for-service providers. Managed care organizations collect vast amounts of data on the costs, processes, and outcomes associated with various diseases, conditions, and treatments. In this new environment, data must be coordinated from patient services delivered in different settings, such as hospitals, clinics, pharmacies, and physician's offices, so that care and payment can be provided efficiently. The result has been a growing number of secondary and tertiary users of personal health information.

Rapidly increasing requirements for the collection, integration, analysis, and storage of health information has resulted in the creation of large scale databases, the capability to link data from distributed databases, and the

---

[96] National Research Council, Computer Science and Telecommunications Board, *For the Record: Protecting Electronic Health Information* (Washington: National Academy Press, 1997), p. 2.

ability for more people in dispersed locations to access data. A variety of mechanisms, both technological and organizational, may be employed to ensure that unauthorized access does not occur and that sufficient audit trails are maintained for proper accountability. Technical measures can be employed to limit access to authorized users for specifically designated purposes. Encryption, the use of smart cards or other unique identifiers for authenticating users, access control software, firewalls to prevent external attacks, and physical security and disaster recovery procedures have all become important elements in creating a technologically secure environment. Computerization has also make it possible to develop approaches for making data anonymous so that individuals cannot be identified. Management practices, including the establishment of strong privacy policies, education and training, and implementing effective sanctions for abuses can contribute substantially to maintaining confidentiality of medical records.

The implementation of the European Union (EU) Data Privacy Directive in October 1998 provided further impetus for congressional action in the $106$th Congress. Article 25 of the directive requires EU member states to enact laws that prohibit the transfer of personal data to non-EU countries that lack an "adequate level of protection." Determinations of adequacy are to be made by the European Commission. If a finding of inadequacy is made, EU member states must block transfers of personal data to that third country. The United States views, with concern, the prohibition on the transfer of data from EU member countries to third countries that do not provide adequate privacy protection. Following two years of discussions with the Europeans, the Department of Commerce recently issued a set of Safe Harbor principles to enable. U.S. companies to meet the "adequacy" requirements of the EU directive.

However, if these developments added impetus for current efforts at legislating medical records privacy, the Health Insurance Portability and Accountability Act of 1996 (HIPAA) provided both impetus and opportunity. The administrative simplification subtitle of the HTPAA instructed the Secretary of Health and Human Services (HHS) to develop standards to support electronic data interchange for a variety of administrative and financial health care transactions. It required the Secretary to issue regulations to establish standard electronic formats for billing and other common transactions, including the use of uniform data codes for reporting diagnoses, referrals, authorizations, and medical procedures. The development of unique identifiers *(i.e.,* identification numbers) for patients, employers, health plans, and health care providers was also mandated. In addition, the subtitle required the Secretary to issue security standards, including an electronic signature standard, to safeguard confidential health information against unauthorized access, disclosure, and misuse.

Finally, the legislation included a timetable for Congress and the Secretary to develop comprehensive medical records privacy standards, which would define the circumstances under which the uses and disclosures of such information require a patient's authorization, and give patients the right to access and amend their personally identifiable health information. The Secretary was required to report to Congress by August 1997 on ways to protect the privacy of personally identifiable health information. It then gave Congress until August 21, 1999, to enact health records privacy legislation. If Congress failed to act, then the Secretary was instructed to issue health records privacy regulations by February 21, 2000.[97]

The Secretary presented her recommendations on health privacy legislation to Congress on September 11, 1997, at a hearing before the Senate Committee on Labor and Human Resources. The recommendations were intended to serve as guidance to Congress in developing comprehensive privacy legislation. The Secretary outlined the following five key principles as being fundamental to the protection of personally identifiable health information.

- Limit, with few exceptions, the use of an individual's health care information to health purposes only.

- Require organizations that are entrusted with health information, including providers and payers, service organizations, organizations receiving information for specified purposes without patient authorization, organizations receiving information pursuant to a patient's authorization, and employers, to provide adequate security measures to protect that information from misuse or disclosure.

- Provide patients with new rights, such as the ability to get copies of records and propose corrections, to control how their health information is used.

---

[97] 110 Stat. 2021; 42 U.S.C. 1320d.

- Hold those who misuse personal health information accountable, and provide redress for persons harmed by its misuse through criminal and civil penalties.

- Balance privacy protections with public responsibility to support national priorities, including public health, research, quality care, and fraud and abuse reduction, which includes allowance of law enforcement access to personal health information in accordance with existing law.[98]

Several health records privacy bills were introduced during 1999, but lawmakers were unable to meet the HIPAA-imposed deadline for enacting comprehensive health privacy legislation. In June 1999, the Senate Committee on Health, Education, Labor, and Pensions (formerly Labor and Human Resources) delayed indefinitely an attempt to mark up a health privacy bill after lawmakers failed to agree on whether to give patients the right to sue over breaches of medical record confidentiality, and whether to allow preemption of all state health privacy laws. With the failure of Congress to meet its self-imposed deadline, the Secretary, on November 3, 1999, issued proposed health records privacy regulations based on the five principles outlined in her report to Congress. The Secretary was unable to propose comprehensive health privacy protections because the HIPAA limits the application of the proposed rule to health plans, health care clearinghouses, and health care providers that maintain and transmit health information electronically.

The proposed health privacy rule gives patients the right to inspect and amend their medical records and requires health plans and providers to obtain a patient's voluntary consent to disclose information, unless the disclosure is related to treating an individual or paying for his or her care. Key provisions of the proposed rule are summarized below.

### *Applicability*

The rule covers health plans, health care providers, and health care clearinghouses, but does not directly apply to other entities that collect and maintain health information. It also covers only information that is electronically transmitted or maintained.

## Individual Rights

Under the proposal, individuals may inspect, copy, and amend their medical records and request restrictions on the use and disclosure of their personally identifiable information in some instances.

## Permitted Uses and Disclosures without Individual Authorization

Personally identifiable information may be used and disclosed for treatment, payment, and health care operations. It may also be used and disclosed for various specified public policy purposes, including research, health care oversight, and law enforcement. All other uses and disclosures require individual authorization. Health plans and health care providers must sign contracts with their business partners that limit how the partners use personally identifiable information.

## Information Practices

Covered entities must disclose the minimum amount of personally identifiable information necessary to fulfill the purpose of the disclosure, and may not condition treatment or payment on obtaining an authorization if one is required. Covered entities must provide up-to-date notice to patients describing their rights and how the entity intends to use personally identifiable information.

## Preemption

The proposed rule preempts state laws that are contrary to, or less protective of, privacy, with some exceptions (e.g., state public health surveillance laws, parental notification laws).

---

[98] See U.S. Congress, Senate Committee on Labor and Human Resources, *Protecting Our Personal Heath Information: Privacy in theElecti-onicAge*, hearings, 105th Cong., 1st sess., Sept. 11 and Oct. 8, 1997 (Washington: GPO, 1998), pp. 21-24.

## Enforcement

The proposed rule provides civil and criminal penalties for non-compliance, but does not give patients the legal right to sue for violations of their health information privacy.[99]

A number of comprehensive health privacy bills were introduced during the 106th Congress. Also, patients' rights legislation, offered in both the House and the Senate, included provisions relating to the confidentiality of health information and the right of individuals to have access to their personal health information. There continues to be general consensus that a federal statute that provides baseline medical records privacy protection would improve safeguards over the existing patchwork of state and federal laws. There also is strong support for a legislative solution to this issue, rather than reliance on federal regulations to protect health privacy rights. The bills introduced during the 106th Congress sought to place restrictions on the use and disclosure of personally identifiable health information, establish security and auditing capabilities for records systems, ensure patients' access to their records, provide the right to seek corrections, require entities to provide notices of their privacy practices, and establish penalties for abuse of privacy rights. The bills varied on the methods for assuring protection, the relationship between federal law and state law, the mechanisms for acquiring informed consent or the use of federal statutes as the basis for allowable disclosures, the rules governing the use of protected health information in conducting research, and procedures for law enforcement access to confidential health information. Finally, the bills also differed in terms of the scope of protected health information covered and the definitions used for such concepts as "non-identifiable health information."

As the 106th Congress moved toward final adjournment, the White House announced in early October that President Clinton was preparing to realize his patient's bill of rights proposal through Department of Labor regulations mandating such guarantees to the 130 million Americans enrolled in private, employer-provided health plans.[100] The regulations were subsequently issued on December 21, 2000, pursuant to the department's authority over employee health benefit and pension benefit programs. In addition to determining medical records disclosure and protection policy, the

---

[99] For information on the development of the Secretarys I-II7PPA health records privacy regulations, including the text of the *FederalRegister* notice and all related public comments, see the HHS Administrative Simplification homepage at Ehttp://aspe.os.dhhs.gov/adnmsimp/index.htm].

[100] Reuters News Agency, "Clinton Moves to Grant Patients Rights," *Washington Times*, Oct. 10, 2000, p. A8.

regulations extend to paper records and oral communications, as well as electronic forms and formats; require patients written consent for even routine disclosure of information; and establish new criminal and civil penalties for health care providers and insurers that impro perly use or disclose medical information. The regulations become fully effective in two years.[101]

## Online Communication

During the past decade, as greater numbers of Americans have explored the Internet, privacy concerns have grown regarding the collection, use, and storage of personal information by website operators. The Clinton Administration and many members of Congress have preferred to rely upon industry self-regulation for realizing privacy protection, but frustration with industry's slow response regarding minors led to the enactment of the Children's Online Privacy Protection Act of 1998, which is profiled above.[102] During the 106th Congress, legislation was offered to address several issues regarding Internet privacy. These included, among others, the responsibilities of Web site operators who collect, use, and store personal information; the extent to which the activities and operations of "individual reference services" or "look-up services" result in personal privacy invasion; online profiling to determine what Web sites are visited by a particular user and the development of a profile of the user's preferences and interests; and the extent to which the personal information storage and transmittal practices of Web site operators contribute to identity theft, in which one individual assumes the identity of another using personal information.[103]

When press disclosures in July 2000 revealed the existence of Carnivore, a new FBI e-mail surveillance system, Congress took immediate interest. The Subcommittee on the Constitution of the House Committee on the Judiciary held a July 24 oversight hearing on Fourth Amendment issues raised by the Carnivore program, receiving testimony from FBI and

---

[101] Associated Press, "Clinton Ensures Privacy for Patients," *Washington Times,* Dec. 20, 2000, p. A4; Associated Press, "New Medical-Privacy RulesCap Almost 10 Years of Debate," *Washington Times,* Dec. 21, 2000, p. A6; Juliet Eilperin, "U.S. Moves to Cloak Medical Records," *Washington Post,* Dec. 20, 2000, pp. Al, A4-A5.
[102] 112 Stat. 2681-728; 15 U.S.C. 6501-6506.
[103] Identity theft is punishable under the Identity Theft and Assumption Deterrence Act of 1998, 112 Stat. 3007.

Department of Justice officials, as well as concerned legal experts and representatives of civil liberties organizations. In early August, the Attorney General announced that an independent review of the Carnivore program and its implications for personal privacy would be conducted, but declined, contrary to the request of 28 Members of Congress, to suspend the program during the interim period before study results were reported.[104] The Senate Committee on the Judiciary reviewed the Carnivore program at a September 6 hearing. In late November, a preliminary draft of the Carnivore study, condticted by the Illinois Institute of Technology Research Institute, found the Internet wiretap program to be a sound law enforcement tool, but recommended some modifications to protect people's routine e-mail and other communications from unlawful interception.[105] Some critics contended that those conducting the study were biased in favor of the new technology, while others argued that biased resulted not only from the selection of the reviewers, but also the ground rules for the study.[106]

At an October 3 Senate Committee on Commerce hearing on proposed legislation to protect the privacy of Internet users (S. 809, S. 2606, and S. 2928), representatives from America Online, Inc. and Hewlett-Packard Company voiced support for a bipartisan proposal introduced by Senator John McCain (R-AZ), the committee chair, and Senator John F. Kerry (D-MA), among others. The measure (S. 2928) would have required Web sites to give online visitors conspicuous notice of their privacy policies, as well as the choice to opt out of efforts to collect data about visitors. Enforcement authority was vested in the Federal Trade Commission. Consumer advocates, however, regarded the bill as too weak. Nonetheless, a consensus prevailed that some legislation was needed, and Senator McCain announced at the end of the proceeding that he would hold more hearings on the online privacy issue in January.[107]

On October 5, both the House and the Senate gave final approval to a conference committee version of legislation (H.R. 4475) appropriating FY2001 funds for the Department of Transportation and related agencies. Among its provisions, Section 501 prohibits agencies funded by Title V of

---

[104] Elisabeth Frater, "Law Enforcement: The Carnivore *Question,"NationalJournal*, vol. 32, Sept. 2, 2000, pp. 2722-2723.

[105] The final version of the evaluation, "Independent Technical Review of the Carnivore System: Final Report," issued December 8, 2000, may be found at the Department of Justice Web site[www.usdoj .gov/jmdlpublications/carniv_final.pdf].

[106] David A. Vise and Dan Eggen, "Study: FBI Tool Needs Honing," *Washington Post*, Nov. 22, 2000, p. A2.

[107] Ariana Eunjung Cha, "Key Firms Back Bill on Web Privacy," *Washington Post*, Oct. 4, 2000, pp. El, El0.

the legislation to use such appropriations (1) to collect, review, or create any aggregate list, derived by any means, that includes the collection of any personally identifiable information relating to an individuals access to or use of any federal government Internet site of the agency, or (2) to enter into any agreement with a third party, including another government agency, to collect, review, or obtain any aggregate list, derived from any means, that includes the collection of any personally identifiable information relating to an individual's access to or use of any nongovernmental Internet site. These limitations do not apply to (1) any record of aggregate data that does not identify particular persons; (2) any voluntary submission of personally identifiable information; (3) any action taken for law enforcement, regulatory, or supervisory purposes, m accordance with applicable law; and (4) any action that is a system security action taken by the operator of an Internet site and is necessarily incident to the rendition of the Internet site services or to the protection of the rights or property of the provider of the Internet site.[108]

The first limitation may be viewed as a response to the June press revelation that the National Drug Control Policy Office, an agency within the Executive Office of the President, was secretly tracking visitors to its Web site through the use of computer software known as "cookies."[109] In response, OMB issued a June 22, 2000, memorandum to the heads of all executive departments and agencies indicating that "'cookies' should not be used at Federal web sites, or by contractors when operating web sites on behalf of agencies, unless, in addition to clear and conspicuous notice, the following conditions are met: a compelling need to gather the data on the site; appropriate and publicly disclosed privacy safeguards for handling of information derived from "cookies"; and personal approval by the head of the agency." The second limitation may be regarded as a response to a September GAO report indicating that, in a survey of online privacy protections at federal Web sites, it had been found that 23 of 70 agencies had disclosed personal information gathered from their websites to third parties—mostly other agencies, but at least four agencies were discovered to

---

[108] See *Congressional Record*, daily edition, vol. 146, Oct. 5, 2000, pp. H8935-H8936, H8980.
[109] See John F. Harris and John Schwartz, "Anti-Drug Web Site Tracks Visitors," *Washington Post*, June 22, 2000, p. A23; Lance Gay, "White House Uses Drug-Message Site to Track Inquiries," *Washington Times*, June 21, 2000, p. A3.

be sharing such information with private sector entities.[110] President Clinton signed the Transportation appropriation bill on October 23, 2000.[111]

Although it began as separate legislation sponsored by several Members in both houses of Congress, the Children's Internet Protection Act was subsequently enacted as Title XVII of the Consolidated Appropriations Act, 2001.[112] The new statute requires schools and libraries that receive "E-rate" discounts, or reduced charges, for Internet access to certify to the Federal Communications Commission that they are using filters to block child pornography and obscene, hard-core pornography sites. Other material, "inappropriate for minors," such as soft-core pornography, may be blocked as well. Opponents of the proposal have contended that it is an unfunded mandate, a federal intrusion into family and local community matters, and a violation of First Amendment guarantees. A court challenge of the new law is anticipated.[113]

## Electronic Commerce

The Convergence of computer and telecommunications technologies has not only revolutionized the storage, retrieval, and sharing of information, but also, in the considered view of many, produced an information economy resulting from commercial transactions on the Internet, both retail business-to-customer and business-to-business in character, which are commonly referred to as electronic commerce or e-commerce. During the past few years, Congress has taken an active interest in e-commerce issues, including some having a bearing upon, or implications for, personal privacy. The utilization of electronic signatures, a means of verifying the identity of a user of a computer system to control access to, or to authorize, a transaction, is one such issue. Legislation Supporting electronic signatures could give them legal status equal to that of written signatures, override the inconsistencies of State law and policies that might hamper or retard the growth of e-commerce, and establish requirements for their use in transactions with the federal government. Just before final adjournment, the 105th Congress

---

[110] Lance Gay, "GAO Finds Agencies Sharing Data of On-line Visitors," *Washington Times,* Sept. 8, 2000, p. A3; U.S. General Accounting Office, *Internet Privacy: Agencies Efforts to Implement OMB 's Privacy Policy,* GAO Report GAO/GGD-00-191 (Washington: September 2000).

[111] P.L. 106-346.

[112] P.L. 106-554.

[113] Cheryl Wetzstein, "New Measure Takes Aim at Obscene Sites on Web," *Washington Times,* Dec. 24, 2000, p. C2.

enacted the Government Paperwork Elimination Act (GPEA) as part of the Omnibus Consolidated and Emergency Supplemental Appropriations Act, 1999.[114] The statute directed OMB to establish procedures for executive branch agencies to accept electronic submissions using electronic signatures, and required them to accept those submissions except where they were found to be impractical or inappropriate. OMB published procedures and guidance for implementing the GPEA on May 2.[115] A July 25, 2000, memorandum from the OMB director to agency chief information officers provides instruction for the preparation and submission of GPEA implementation plans to OIRA.[116]

The 106th Congress enacted the Electronic Signatures in Global and National Commerce Act in June 2000.[117] The statute, dubbed E-SIGN, promotes the use of electronic signatures, contract formation, and record-keeping in private commerce by establishing legal equivalence between contracts in paper or electronic form, pen-and-ink and electronic signatures, and other legally-required written documents and the same information in electronic form. It applies broadly to commercial, consumer and business transactions in or affecting interstate or foreign commerce, and to transactions regulated by both federal and state government. OMB draft procedures and guidance for implementing the E-SIGN were circulated within the executive branch for comment on August 3 with a closure date of August 11. The E-SIGN became effective on October 1, 2000.

These initiatives promoting the use of electronic signatures in e-commerce have raised some personal privacy issues. For example, the initial procedures and guidance OMB proposed for implementing the GPEA prompted Concerns for some privacy advocacy groups that a reliance on using personal information to establish one s identity was being created, with the result that, as a consequence of its collection by the federal government and federal contractors, larger holdings of such information would be realized. Also, some urge that more attention be given to the danger of identity theft resulting from electronic signatures being stolen or sold by unauthorized persons, a privacy invasion portending a variety of legal and financial problems for the victims.

---

[114] 112 Stat. 2681-749.
[115] *Federal Register,* vol. 65, May 2, 2000, pp. *25508-25521.*
[116] This memorandum is available in the "Information Policy and Technology" section of the OMB Web site at [http://www.whitehousegov/OMB/infore~indexh~]
[117] 114 Stat. 464.

Encryption, the encoding and decoding of electronic messages through the use of "keys" to communicate sensitive information and data, is another important aspect of e-commerce development. At the core of the congressional debate on this subject is the issue of who holds the keys. The 105$^{th}$ Congress considered several bills addressing national encryption policy, but none was enacted, and the controversy continued into the 106$^{th}$ Congress. Initially, the Clinton Administration favored a policy of the federal government holding the encryption keys for major commercial transactions. When industry and congressional critics contended that this arrangement could easily result in violations of citizen's privacy rights, the administration shifted to a policy of having a "spare key" held by a third party "key recovery agent," and not directly held by the federal government. Critics remained uncomfortable with the prospect of the federal government ultimately having access to the "spare key" for law enforcement and national security purposes. Other factors under consideration are liability protection for proper release of keys and penalties for improper use or release of keys. Congressional discussion and exploration of national encryption policy continues.

Another e-commerce issue under congressional consideration is the regulation of unsolicited commercial e-mail (UCE), sometimes referred to as "spam" or "junk e-mail." There are several dimensions to the issue, including the question of UCE qualifying as a form of commercial speech that is protected by the First Amendment, the perpetration of fraud, and the matter of UCE cost being passed on to consumers through higher charges from Internet service providers who must upgrade their systems to handle the increased traffic. Also, for some, the intrusiveness of UCE constitutes an invasion of privacy. Congress enacted a statue in 1991; the Telephone Consumer Protection Act, that required the Federal Communications Commission to prohibit unsolicited calls from automatic dialing devices that played a recorded message to all private residences and police, fire, and other emergency lines, and also banned the automatic calls from facsimile machines that transmitted unsolicited marketing materials via the telephone lines.[118] Whether there should be an analogous law for regulating UCE, or a requirement that would allow a consumer, before opening an e-mail message, to determine whether or not it is unsolicited advertising and to direct the sender to cease transmissions of such messages, remains under congressional consideration.

---

[118] 105 Stat. 2394; 47 U.S.C. 227.

Finally, an attempt to protect personal privacy by prohibiting the public display of an individual's Social Security number for commercial purposes without consent became embroiled in controversy in the closing days of the 106~ Congress. Legislation on this matter was introduced by Senator Judd Gregg (R-NH) on May 15, 2000 (S. 2554). It was denominated Amy Boyers Law in memory of a New Hampshire woman who was slain by a man who tracked her down after buying her Social Security number on the Internet. A modified version of the proposal was subsequently attached in the Senate to legislation appropriating finds for the Departments of Commerce, Justice, and State and related agencies for FY2001 (H.R. 4690). Critics of the modified version reportedly contended it was a Trojan Horse because exceptions to the proposals regulatory arrangements allowed giant data brokers, banks, marketers and private detectives to exchange or sell Social Security numbers among themselves.[119] In an October 26 letter to the House and Senate leadership, President Clinton expressed "serious concerns" about several provisions of the Commerce, Justice, State appropriations bill, saying, at one point:

> The bill fails to address in any meaningful way the real privacy concerns about Social Security numbers raised by the Administration. Regrettably, it does not include needed protections against the inappropriate sale and display of individual citizens Social Security numbers. Moreover, tile bill creates loopholes that seriously undermine the goal of the legislation to protect privacy.[120]

The bill was not immediately presented to the President and conferees subsequently agreed to remove the section.[121]

For additional information concerning personal privacy issues receiving congressional consideration, consult the relevant CRS products identified in the reading list at the end of this report.

---

[119] Robert O. Harrow, Jr., "New Privacy Bill Called 'Trojan Horse,'" Washington Post, Oct. 25, 2000, pp. El, E6.

[120] White House, Office of the Press Secretary, *Text of a Letter from the President to the Speaker of the House of Representatives, the Majority Leader of the Senate, and the Democratic Leaders of the House and Senate* (Washington: Oct. 26, 2000), available from the Virtual Library at [http://www.whitehouse.gov].

[121] See the supplemental explanatory statement in *Congressional Record,* daily edition, vol. 146, Dec. 15, 2000, p. H12481 (indicating no conference agreement on section

## FOR FURTHER READING

CRS Report RS20026, *Banking s Proposed "Know Your Customer" Rules,* by M. Maureen Murphy

CR8 Report RS20426, *Electronic Commerce: An Introduction,* by Glenn J. McLoughlin.

CRS Report RS20344, *Electronic Signatures: Technology Developments and Legislative Issues,* by Richard M. Nunno.

CRS Issue Brief 1B96039, *Encryption Technology: Congressional Issues,* by Richard M. Nunno.

CRS Report 94-980, *Family Educational Rights and Privacy Act: P.L. 1 03-382 Amendments,* by Richard N. Apling.

CRS Report RL30620, *Health Information Security and Privacy: HJPAA and Proposed Implementing Regulations,* by S. Stephen Redhead.

CRS Report 98-67, *Internet: An Overview of Key Technology Policy Issues Affecting Its Use and Growth,* by Marcia S. Smith, Richard M. Nunno, John D. Moteff, and Leonard G. Kruger.

CRS Report RL30784, *Internet Privacy: An Analysis of Technology and Policy Issues,* by Marcia S. Smith.

CRS Report *RS20035, Internet Privacy—Protecting Personal Information: Overview and Pending Legislation,* by Marcia S. Smith.

CRS Report RS20037, *"Junk Mail": An Overview of Issues and Legislation Concerning Unsolicited Commercial Electronic Mail ("Spain"),* by Marcia S. Smith.

CRS Report RL30375, *Major Financial Services Legislation, The Gramm-Leach-Bliley Act (P.L. 106-1 02): An Overview,* by F. Jean Wells and William D. Jackson.

CRS Issue Brief 1B98002, *Medical Records Confidentiality,* by C. Stephen Redhead, Harold C. Relyea, and Gina Marie Stevens.

CRS Report RS20500, *Medical Records Privacy: Questions and Answers on the Proposed Federal Regulations,* by C. Stephen Redhead.

CRS Report RS20185, *Privacy Protection for Customer Financial Information,* by Maureen Murphy.

CRS Report RL30477, *Summary of the Proposed Rule for the Privacy of Individually Identifiable Health Information,* by Gina Marie Stevens and Melinda DeAtley.

---

*635* of H.R. *5548* as appended to H.R. 4942 in conference; see *Congressional Record,* daily edition, Oct. 25, 2000, p. H11143).

CRS Report 96-233. *The Telecommunications Act of .7996 (FL. 104-104): A Brief Overview*, by Angele A. Gilroy.

CRS Report RS20509, *Trends in the Financial Services Industry: Online Banking and Payments*, by F. Jean Wells.

# THE FOURTH AMENDMENT
# A CHANGING LANDSCAPE

## *Elizabeth B. Bazan*

### INTRODUCTION

In this report, the recent evolution of Fourth Amendment law will be examined through the vehicle of U.S. Supreme Court decisions. The Fourth Amendment provides:

> The right of the people to be secure in their persons, houses, papers, and effects, against unreasonable searches and seizures, shall not be violated; and no Warrants shall issue but upon probable cause, supported by Oath or affirmation, and particularly describing the place to be searched, and the persons or things to be seized.

The development of the Fourth Amendment, while building upon British experience,[1] drew its impetus from the colonial experience with the so-called "writs of assistance," general warrants used by the English authorities to enforce revenue laws, These general warrants gave those who bore them the power to go into any house or place to search for prohibited and uncustomed goods and to seize such items. Further, the writs of assistance directed all subjects to assist in such efforts. The writs were not of short duration, but

---

[1] *See, e.g., Semayne's Case,* 5 Coke's Repts. 91a, 77 Eng. Rep. 194 (KB 1604); *Entick v. Carrington,* 19 Howell's State Trials 1029, 95 Eng. 807 (1705).

rather continued in force until six months after the death of the sovereign who issued them.[2]

This Amendment protects against unreasonable official incursions into privacy interests, protecting both property interests from unreasonable searches and seizures, and any interests of the person, which may be unreasonably impinged upon incident to seizures such as arrests and investigatory stops. The Supreme Court's decisions in recent terms have significantly altered the legal parameters of Fourth Amendment protections, in many instances circumscribing the reach of those protections. This report will focus on the Court's Fourth Amendment decisions from the 1988 Term to the present. Among the issues which will be addressed are those which deal with inventory searches of closed containers in vehicles impounded incident to an arrest, as well as warrantless and consent searches of closed containers in vehicles; developments related to the plain view doctrine; aerial searches; employee drug testing; sobriety checkpoints; and extraterritorial application of the Fourth Amendment's search and seizure protections. Other cases address warrantless felony arrests in the suspect's home with probable cause, new developments relating to investigatory stops, the use of excessive force to effect a seizure in the form of an investigatory stop or of an arrest, and an application of the impeachment exception to the exclusionary rule. Still others deal with the application of the Fourth Amendment reasonableness standard to the permissible length of detention prior to a probable cause determination hearing, and the applicability of the exclusionary rule to evidence discarded by a fleeing suspect prior to his capture. As is apparent from the diversity of issues to be examined, the Court continues to play an active role in refining and redefining the reach of the Fourth Amendment's role in criminal proceedings end administrative contexts.

Traditionally, the Court has often read the Fourth Amendment as requiring a warrant for a search or a seizure (a term read broadly enough to cover an arrest), unless the circumstances involved fell into a narrow group of exceptions. However, recently this approach has sometimes given way to the application of an approach, which focused on a determination of whether the search or arrest was reasonable under the circumstances involved. One might view these differing approaches as turning upon whether the Fourth Amendment is to be read in toto, the requirement for warrants based upon

---

[2] For further discussion of the writs of assistance and of English experiences which laid the foundation for the Fourth Amendment, see *The Constitution of the United States of America, Analysis and Interpretation*, S. Doc. 99-16, 99th Cong., 1st Sess. 1155-1157 (1987) (hereinafter *Constitution Annotated*).

probable cause being seen as defining the standard for reasonable searches or seizures, including arrests; or whether these two clauses are to be read in the alternative, with those searches or arrests made incident to a warrant requiring probable cause, but anticipating that other searches or seizures might occur which would be reasonable without recourse to a warrant.[3]

In recent case law, the Court appears to be articulating a general rule that searches and seizures must be pursuant to a warrant supported by probable cause, while significantly expanding the number and scope of the exceptions to the warrant requirement in the Fourth Amendment, and measuring the cases that fall within those exceptions by a reasonableness test. In the latter set of circumstances, the Court is increasingly looking at whether the person raising the Fourth Amendment argument had a reasonable expectation of privacy, which was subjected to a governmental intrusion, and whether that intrusion was justifiable.[4] For example, one area where the Court has articulated the general rule then applied the reasonableness standard to an exception which has broad ramifications is that of administrative searches which fall within the category of "special needs beyond the normal need for law enforcement." *National Treasury Employees Union v. Von Raab*, 109 S. Ct. 1384, 1390 (1989) (drug testing of employees). The Court appears to be applying a balancing test in such cases, balancing the degree of intrusion into Fourth Amendment protected interests against the governmental interest sought to be furthered. Where such balancing has occurred, the governmental interest has generally been found to prevail.[5]

---

[3] See, e.g., Marron v. United States, 275 U.S. 192(1927); *Go-Bart Importing Co. v. United States* 282 U.S. 344 (1931); Harris v, United States, 331 U.S. 145 (1947); *Chime! v. California*, 395 U.S. 752 (1969); *Maryland v. Buie*, 110 S. Ct. 1093 (1990); *New York v. Harris*, 110 S. Ct. 1460 (1990); *Horton v. California*, 110 S. Ct. 2301 (1990).

[4] See, e.g., Florida v. Riley, 109 S. Ct. 693, 695-97 (1989); California V. Ciraolo, 476 U.S. 207 (1986) (both dealing with aerial searches); Skinner v. Railway Labor Executives Assn., 109 5. Ct. 1402, 1412-13 (1989); *National Treasury Employees Union v. Von Raab*, 109 S. Ct. 1384, 1390-92 (1989) (both dealing with drug testing of employees, in circumstances "where a Fourth Amendment intrusion serves special governmental needs, beyond the normal need for law enforcement. In such cases, the Court requires a balancing of the individual's privacy expectations against the Government's interests to determine whether it is impractical to require a warrant or some level of individualized suspicion in the particular context." *National Treasury Employees Union, supra,* 109 S. Ct. at 1390. In each case, the Court found the governmental interest overrode the personal privacy interests involved.).

[5] *See, e.g., Michigan Dept of State Police v. Sitz,* 110 S. Ct. 2481 (1990) (finding sobriety checkpoints where vehicles are briefly stopped without individualized suspicion of wrongdoing constitutional under Fourth Amendment standards); *National Treasury*

One area where such a balancing of interests is apparent is in the area of investigatory stops. There the Court has held that such stops may be made in the absence of a warrant and on less than probable cause, so long as they are supported by reasonable suspicion of criminal wrongdoing based upon articulable facts. The case which set the cornerstone for the development of Fourth Amendment doctrine in this area was *Terry v. Ohio,* 392 U.S. 1 (1968). *Terry* involved a stop and frisk situation. In that case, a police officer observed three individuals conducting themselves in a manner, which, based upon the officer's experience, appeared to indicate that the individuals were "casing" a store as an armed robbery target. The officer stopped the individuals, and identified himself, but did not receive prompt identification by the men. The officer then seized one of the men and patted down the exterior of his clothes in search of weapons. In the course of this, the officer found a gun, The Court found Fourth Amendment rights implicated in this situation, where "a police officer accosts an individual and restrains his freedom to walk away." *Id.,* at 16. The Court applied a reasonableness test, looking to whether the officer could point to "specific and articulable facts which, taken together with rational inferences from those facts" that a neutral magistrate would conclude would lead a man of reasonable caution to believe that possible criminal conduct was involved and that an investigative stop and a frisk were warranted. *Id.,* at 20-22. This case and its progeny gave rise to the requirement of a reasonable suspicion of criminal activity for an investigative stop. The Court's analysis in these cases has been very fact specific, examining the totality of the circumstances, and requiring the officer to have articulable reasons or founded suspicions upon which to base his reasonable suspicion of criminal activity.[6]

---

*Employees Union, supra,* 109 S. Ct., at 1390; *Skinner v. Railway Labor Executives Assn.,* 109 S. Ct, 1402 (1989); *New Jersey v. T.L.O.,* 469 U.S. 325 (1985) (search of student's person and effects by school authorities based upon reasonable grounds that the search will demonstrate violations of law or school rules); *Griffin v, Wisconsin,* 483 U.S. 868 (1987) (warrantless searches of probationers home based on less than probable cause not violative of Fourth Amendment); *O'Connor v. Ortega,* 480 U.S. 709 (1987) (applying reasonableness standard to work-related searches of government employees offices by employer). *Cf., Hudson v. Palmer,* 468 U.S. 517 (1984) (Fourth Amendment protections do not extend to searches of prison cell).

[6] *See, e.g., Alabama u. White,* 110 S. Ct, 2412 (1990) (anonymous tip corroborated by independent police work has indicia of reliability to provide reasonable suspicion for an investigatory stop); *United States v. Sokolow,* 109 S. Ct. 1581 (1989) (drug courier profile); *United States u. Carte;* 449 U.S. 411 (1981); *United States v. Mendehhall,* 446 U.S. 544 (1980).

While this discussion is far from exhaustive, it will provide a general background through which an examination of the Fourth Amendment cases of the 1988, 1989 and 1990 Terms can be placed in context.

## INVESTIGATIVE STOPS

The Court considered two cases involving investigative stops in the operative time period. As noted above, the case law in this area flows from the Court's decision in *Terry v. Ohio*, 392 U.S. 1 (1968), where the Court held that the police can stop and briefly detain a person for investigative purposes if the officer has a reasonable suspicion supported by articulable facts that suggest current or impending criminal activity. The officer need not have probable cause to support the stop. *Id.*, at 30.

In *Alabama v. White*, 110 S. Ct. 2412 (1990), the Court found that an anonymous tip, corroborated by independent police work, had sufficient indicia of reliability to support an investigatory stop without offending Fourth Amendment standards. The corroboration involved was not totally independent of the anonymous tip. Rather, the corroboration stemmed purely from the police surveillance of White acting as the tip had indicated that she would. The case arose out of an anonymous telephone tip which indicated that White would leave a specified apartment at a set time in a specified vehicle, that she would go to a particular motel, and that she would possess cocaine at the time, White was put under police surveillance. This observation showed that White did leave the apartment building and drive most of the way to the motel. She was stopped at that time. A consensual search of the car she was driving uncovered marijuana. She was placed under arrest. A search of her purse incident to her arrest revealed cocaine. The Court found that the tip, plus the results of the police surveillance, created a reasonable suspicion of criminal activity sufficient to pass Fourth Amendment muster in connection with an investigative stop.

In *United States u. Sokolow*, 109 S. Ct. 1581 (1989), the Court examined the question of whether the use of a Drug Enforcement Administration (DEA) drug courier profile as a basis for evaluating a suspect's behavior was sufficient to provide a reasonable suspicion, based upon articulable *facts*, that criminal activity was present so as to justify a *Terry* stop. While recognizing that many of the individual aspects of the behavior at issue could be completely consistent with the behavior of an innocent traveler, the Court concluded that constitutional standards had been met. The information in the hands of the DEA agents at the time of the stop demonstrated that the defendant had bought two airplane tickets, costing $2,100, in cash from a roll of $20 bills; that he traveled under an assumed name; that his original destination was *Miami,* which was a source city for illegal narcotics; that he stayed in Miami two days, despite the fact that the flight from Honolulu to Miami was 20 hours long; that he seemed nervous during his trip; and that he did not check his luggage. 109 S. Ct., at 1583. The Court found this series of facts provided a basis for a reasonable suspicion of ongoing or imminent criminal activity. Further, the Court found that the fact that they could be set out in a profile did not alter their evidentiary significance when seen by a trained agent. *Id.,* at 1587.

## POLICE QUESTIONING AND LUGGAGE SEARCH ON A BUS

The Court's most recent Fourth Amendment decision, in *Florida v. Bostick,* No. 89-1717, slip op. (U.S., June 20, 1991), contrasts with the previous two cases discussed in that it involved police questioning of a bus passenger at a scheduled stop, without reasonable suspicion or probable cause to suspect criminal activity was afoot. While the facts of the case were disputed, as the Florida Supreme Court described them, two police officers wearing insignia, one of whom carried a gun in a zipper pouch, boarded a bus during a stopover. Without reasonable suspicion based upon articulable facts, the officers picked out Bostick and asked for his ticket and identification. Having found these in order and having returned them to Bostick, the officers identified themselves as narcotics agents and asked Bostick's consent to search his luggage. Although the point was disputed, the state trial judge found that the defendant was advised of his right to refuse this request, and he consented to the search. Contraband was found in the luggage. The majority of the Court found that the officers did not threaten Bostick with a gun, analogizing the carrying of the zippered pouch to the carrying of a gun in its holster. Defendant moved to suppress the evidence of the search, but his motion was denied without factual findings. While entering a guilty plea, Bostick reserved the right to appeal this denial. The Florida District Court of Appeal affirmed, but certified the question to the Florida Supreme Court. That court announced a per se rule that foreclosed the police from doing drug searches on buses during scheduled stops and from questioning passengers without articulable reasons for doing so and thereby gaining their consent to search their luggage.

The U.S. Supreme Court framed the question before it as being "whether a police encounter on a bus of the type described above necessarily constitutes a "seizure" within the meaning of the Fourth Amendment." *Id.,* slip op. at 4. In the Court's view, this question was premised upon the assumption that the police did not meet the reasonable suspicion standard to justify a seizure, and further, that if there was a seizure, the drugs seized would have to be suppressed as fruit of a tainted search. The Court noted that police questioning, alone, does not constitute a search, and that a consensual encounter akin to the one at issue, had it occurred in a lobby or bus terminal, would not amount to a seizure. Bostick argued that the cramped confines of the bus distinguished his case from similar encounters in more open settings. The majority of the Court disagreed. The Court noted that here Bostick's freedom of movement was restricted by the fact that he was a passenger on a bus, a factor independent of the police actions. Therefore, the pertinent inquiry, in the Court's view, was not whether Bostick felt free to leave, but rather whether a reasonable person would feel free to terminate the encounter; whether, in light of all of the surrounding circumstances, "the police conduct would 'have communicated to a reasonable person that he was not at liberty to ignore the police presence and go about his business... Where the encounter takes place is one factor, but it is not the only one." *Id.,* slip op. at 7. The Court further noted that "an individual may decline an officer's request without fearing prosecution.... We have consistently held that a refusal to cooperate, without more, does not furnish the minimal level of objective justification needed for a detention or seizure." *Id.* Justice O'Connor, writing for the majority, articulated the standard to be applied as follows:

> We adhere to the rule that, in order to determine whether a particular encounter constitutes a seizure, a court must consider all the circumstances surrounding the encounter to determine whether the police conduct would have communicated to a reasonable person that the person was not free to decline the officers' requests or otherwise terminate the encounter. That rule applies to encounters that take place on a city street or in an airport lobby, and it applies equally to encounters on a bus. The Florida Supreme Court erred in adopting a per se rule.

*Id.,* slip op. at 10. The Court did not decide whether or not a seizure occurred in the case before it. Rather, the Court reversed the decision of the Florida

Supreme Court and remanded for further proceedings not inconsistent with the *Bostick* opinion.

## SOBRIETY CHECKPOINTS

The sobriety checkpoint case, *Michigan Department of State Police v. Sitz,* 110 S. Ct. 2481 (1990), provides an interesting counterpoint to the last three cases. In *Sitz,* the Court concluded that a seizure for Fourth Amendment purposes occurred when a vehicle was stopped at a sobriety checkpoint. Applying a balancing test, the Court balanced the State's interest in preventing drunk driving, and the extent to which the checkpoint system could reasonably be said to advance that interest, against the degree of intrusion upon individual motorists who are stopped briefly at those checkpoints. In the Court's view, the governmental interests prevailed, and the checkpoint system at issue was deemed consistent with Fourth Amendment requirements. In reaching this conclusion, the Court rejected an argument that a showing of special governmental need beyond the normal need for Law enforcement must be satisfied before a balancing test can be applied. The Court analogized instead to the balancing test it applied in *United States v. Martinez-Fuerte,* 428 U.S. 543 (1976), in approving highway checkpoints used to detect illegal aliens, and in its decision in *Brown v. Texas,* 443 U.S. 47 (1979), in holding unconstitutional the detention of an individual for purposes of identification without reasonable suspicion of criminal activity.

In *Martinez-Fuerte,* the Court considered the constitutional sufficiency of brief stops of vehicles to question their occupants at permanent checkpoints operated by the Border Patrol away from the international border with Mexico, where those stops were not supported by probable cause or reasonable suspicion of illegal activity. The Court did not require that the operation of such fixed checkpoints be authorized in advance by a warrant. In finding the fixed checkpoints constitutionally permissible, the Court noted that the need for these routine checkpoints was great, set on major highways to stem the flow of illegal aliens, while the intrusion into Fourth Amendment interests was "quite limited." 428 U.S., at 557. Neither the occupants nor the vehicles were searched. Rather, the officers conducted a visual inspection of each car and asked a few questions of the vehicle's occupants and, at times, requested documentation reflecting a right to be in the United States. This system was perceived as less likely to be frightening or annoying to motorists than roving checkpoints. The Court observed further that the degree of potential interference with legitimate traffic by fixed checkpoints was minimal. The Court pointed out that checks were routine and involved limited discretion on the part of those enforcing the checkpoints, minimizing the opportunity for abusive or arbitrary actions. In thus balancing the degree of intrusion against the governmental needs, the Court found that Fourth Amendment proscriptions were not violated by the fixed checkpoints at issue.

In *Brown*, the Court found the detention of the appellant to require him to identify himself constituted a seizure under the Fourth Amendment. In analyzing the reasonableness of such a seizure, the Court sought to balance the

> . . .public interest against the individual's right to personal security free from arbitrary interference by law officers. ... Consideration of the constitutionality of such seizures involves the weighing of the gravity of the public concerns served by the seizure, the degree to which the seizure advances the public interest, and the severity of the interference with individual liberty.
> A central concern in balancing these competing considerations in a variety of settings has been to assure that an individual's reasonable expectation of privacy is not subject to arbitrary invasions solely at the unfettered discretion of the officers in the field. . . . To this end, the Fourth Amendment requires that a seizure must be based on specific, objective facts indicating that society's legitimate interests require the seizure of the particular individual, or that the seizure must be carried out pursuant to a plan embodying explicit, neutral limitations on the conduct of individual officers....
> 
> 443 U.S., at 50-51.

The *Brown* Court found that the detention of the individual in the case at bar was not supported by any objective facts giving rise to a reasonable suspicion that he was engaged in criminal activity. The Texas statute under which the detention for identification purposes took place was found to have been unconstitutionally applied in this case. A stop without the underlying foundation of objective facts opened the door to potentially arbitrary and abusive police conduct. "In the absence of any basis for suspecting appellant of misconduct, the balance between the public interest and the appellant's right to personal security and privacy tilts in favor of freedom from police interference." *Id.*, at 52.

## CHASING A FLEEING SUSPECT

In contrast to *Brown,* the Court in *California v. Hodari 12.,* No. 89-1632, slip op. (U.S., April 23, 1991), found that a seizure had not yet occurred when a police officer gave chase to a fleeing juvenile suspect. The case arose out of the flight of a group of youths, including Hodari D., when an unmarked police car approached them. An officer, wearing a jacket, which identified him as a police officer, pursued Hodari D. Rather than following him directly, the officer took a route, which permitted him to intercept Hodari D. When the juvenile suspect saw the officer, the suspect threw a small rock away. The officer then tackled him. The discarded rock was recovered by police and determined to be crack cocaine. The lower court, in the juvenile proceeding rejected Hodari D.'s motion to suppress the cocaine. The state appellate court determined that the cocaine should have been excluded from evidence on the theory that Hodari D. had been seized at the time the officer gave chase, and that the seizure was unreasonable because it was not founded upon reasonable suspicion of criminal wrongdoing. The U.S. Supreme Court disagreed, concluding that Hodari D. had not been seized for Fourth Amendment purposes at the time the cocaine was discarded, and that the cocaine could therefore be used in evidence against the defendant in juvenile proceedings.

## USE OF EXCESSIVE OR DEADLY FORCE

The reasonableness of a seizure is also the operative consideration in cases involving allegations of excessive force. In *Brower* p. *County of Inyo,* 109 S. Ct. 1378 (1989), a Fourth Amendment seizure issue arose in the context of a suit brought by Brower's estate under 42 U.S.C. § 1983. The Court held that a Fourth Amendment seizure occurred where a governmental termination of a person's movement was achieved through means intentionally applied by the Government to that end. In the case at bar, Brower was killed when the stolen car he was driving in a high-speed chase, seeking to elude the police, collided with an 18-wheel truck placed across the road by the police to stop him. The plaintiffs in the suit alleged that this had been done in a constitutionally deficient and unreasonable manner, because the truck was placed without illumination, beyond a curve in the road, with police lights shining into the eyes of the oncoming driver, blinding him to the presence of the truck. The Fourth Amendment claim had been dismissed by the court below for failure to state a claim upon which relief could be granted. The Supreme Court reversed and remanded the case for further proceedings.

The finding that the alleged police misconduct would amount to a Fourth Amendment seizure appears consistent with the Court's 1985 decision in *Tennessee v. Garner,* 471 U.S. 1 (1985). There the Court held, in part, that the fatal shooting of a fleeing suspect by a police officer constituted a seizure for Fourth Amendment purposes. *Id.,* at 7. In *Garner,* the Court applied a Fourth Amendment analysis to the issue of whether the use of deadly force to prevent the escape of an apparently unarmed suspected felon was unconstitutional. *Id.* at 3. The Court found "that such force may not be used unless it is necessary to prevent the escape and the officer has probable cause to believe that the suspect poses a significant threat of death or serious physical injury to the officer or others." *Id.* In *Garner,* a police officer identified himself as such and ordered an apparently unarmed, slight, young burglary suspect to halt. When he continued to flee, the officer, acting under the authority of a state law and police departmental policy, shot and killed the suspect.

In concluding that the use of deadly force constituted a seizure, the Court distinguished between the requirement that probable cause exist before an arrest may be made and the necessity that the manner in which any seizure, including an arrest, is made must be reasonable. Again, the Court applied a balancing test in assessing the constitutional sufficiency of the seizure, balancing

> "... the nature and quality of the intrusion on the individual's Fourth Amendment interests against the importance of the governmental interests alleged to justify the intrusion." . . . Because one of the factors is the extent of the intrusion, it is plain that reasonableness depends on not only when a seizure is made, but also how it is carried out....
> ... In each of these cases, the question was whether the totality of the circumstances justified a particular sort of search or seizure.

*Id.,* at 8-9. In applying this balancing test to the use of deadly force in apprehending a suspect, the Court stated:

> The same balancing process applied in the cases cited above demonstrates that, notwithstanding probable cause to seize a suspect, an officer may not always do so by killing him. The intrusiveness of a seizure by means of deadly force is unmatched. The suspect's fundamental interest in his own

life need not be elaborated upon. The use of deadly force also frustrated the interest of the individual, and of society, in judicial determination of guilt and punishment. Against these interests are ranged governmental interests in effective law enforcement. It is argued that overall violence will be reduced by encouraging the peaceful submission of suspects who know that they may be shot if they flee....

Without in any way disparaging the importance of these goals, we are not convinced that the use of deadly force is a sufficiently productive means of accomplishing them to justify the killing of nonviolent suspects... The use of deadly force is a self-defeating way of apprehending a suspect and so *setting* the criminal justice mechanism in motion. If successful, it guarantees that that mechanism will not be set in motion. And while the meaningful threat of deadly force might be thought to lead to the arrest of more live suspects by discouraging escape attempts, the presently available evidence does not support this thesis.... Petitioners and appellant have not persuaded us that shooting nondangerous fleeing suspects is so vital as to outweigh the suspect's interest in his own life.

*Id.,* at 9-11.

The *Garner* Court found that the Fourth Amendment reasonableness standard was not satisfied by the use of deadly force to prevent the escape of all felony suspects, regardless of the particular circumstances involved. The Court found that where a suspect was "unarmed" and "nondangerous," posing "no immediate threat to the officer and no threat to others, the harm resulting from failing to apprehend him does not justify the use of deadly force to do so." *Id.,* at 11. On the other hand,

if the suspect threatens the officer with a weapon or there is probable cause to believe that he has committed a crime involving the infliction or threatened infliction of serious physical harm, deadly force may be used if necessary to prevent escape, and if, where feasible, some warning has been given....

*Id.,* at 11-12.

The application of the Fourth Amendment reasonableness standard was also the focus of the Court's attention in *Graham v, Connor,* 109 S. Ct. 1865 (1989). There the Court held that the constitutional standard which "governs a free citizen's claim that law enforcement officials used excessive force in the course of making an arrest, investigatory stop, or other 'seizure' of his persona was the "Fourth Amendment's 'objective reasonableness' standard, rather than ... a substantive due process standard." 109 S. Ct., at 1867. This case involved an action under 42 U.S.C.§ 1983 to recover damages for injuries, which were allegedly sustained because of the use of physical force by police officers conducting an investigatory stop. Graham's injuries included a broken foot, cuts on his wrists, a bruised forehead, and an injured shoulder, along with a persistent ringing in one ear. The stop arose when the police observed Graham, a diabetic, quickly enter and leave a convenience store to which a friend had driven him. He sought orange juice there to counteract an insulin reaction, but the line at the store was too long for him to wait. He reentered his friend's car and asked to be driven to a friend's house. Police stopped them nearby, detaining them while the officer determined whether anything amiss had occurred at the convenience store, although the officer was advised that Graham was suffering from "a sugar reaction."

Graham alleged, in essence, that the police used excessive force against him during the investigatory stop, refused to listen to an explanation of his medical condition, and refused proffered orange juice from one of Graham's friends, which would have counteracted the insulin reaction he was experiencing during the stop. The district court had directed a verdict in favor of the respondents, and, therefore, against Graham, using a four-factor substantive due process test derived from *Johnson v. Glick*, 481 F.2d 1028 (2d Cir.), *cert. denied,* 414 U.S. 1033 (1973), to analyze the excessive force claim. This was affirmed by a divided court of appeals. The Supreme Court reversed, rejecting the contention that all excessive force claims arising under Section 1983 were to be tested under the same generic standard. Rather, the Court concluded that one must first determine what constitutional right has been allegedly infringed by the use of excessive force in a given case, typically either the Fourth Amendment right to be free from unreasonable seizures or the Eighth Amendment prohibition against cruel and unusual punishment. Then the test appropriate to the right infringed should be applied. In the context of an "arrest or investigatory stop of a free citizen," the Fourth Amendment reasonableness standard is implicated. To apply it, one must look to both when the seizure was made and how it was carried out. 109 S. Ct., at 1870-71. Such an examination would include consideration of the "severity of the crime at issue, whether the suspect poses an immediate threat to the safety of the officers or others, and whether he is actively resisting arrest or attempting to evade arrest by flight," *Id.,* at 1872, *citing Garner, supra.* The operative inquiry must be into whether "the officers actions are 'objectively reasonable' in light of the facts and circumstances confronting them, without regard to their underlying motivation." *Id.*, at 1872. Thus, the "'reasonableness' of a particular use of force must be judged from the perspective of a reasonable officer on the scene, rather than with the 20/20 vision of hindsight." *Id.* In making such a determination, allowance must be made "for the fact that police officers are often forced to make split-second judgments--in circumstances that are tense, uncertain, and rapidly evolving--about the amount of force that is necessary in a particular situation," *Id.*

## DETENTION BEFORE PROBABLE CAUSE HEARING

The reasonableness of the length of a period of detention prior to a hearing to determine whether probable cause existed to support a warrantless arrest was the subject of the Court's scrutiny in *County of Riverside v. McLaughlin,* No. 89-1817, slip op. (U.S., May 13, 1991). In this case, McLaughlin brought a class action seeking injunctive and declaratory relief under 42 U.S.C. § 1983 for the county's failure to hold a probable cause hearing promptly. The Court relied on its decision in *Gerstein v. Pugh,* 420 U.S. 108 (1975), in reaching its decision. The *Gerstein* Court held, in part, "that the Fourth Amendment requires a prompt judicial determination of probable cause as a prerequisite to an extended pretrial detention following a warrantless arrest. *McLaughlin, supra,* slip op. at 1, *citing Gerstein, supra.* The *McLaughlin* Court clarified the concept of "prompt" in this context. The *Gerstein* Court left the states latitude to choose the procedures and mechanisms by which they met the constitutional requirement of prompt judicial determination of probable cause issues. It permitted probable cause determinations to be combined with other pre—trial procedures, such as arraignment. In *McLaughlin,* the Court stated that:

> ... flexibility has its limits; *Gerstein* is not a blank check. A State has no legitimate interest in detaining for extended periods individuals who have been arrested without probable cause. The Court recognized in *Gerstein* that a person arrested without a warrant is entitled to a fair and reliable determination of probable cause and that this determination must be made promptly.
> ...
> Out task in this case is to articulate more clearly the boundaries of what is permissible under the Fourth Amendment. Although we hesitate to announce that the Constitution compels a specific time limit, it is important to provide some degree of certainty so the States and counties may establish procedures with confidence that they fall within constitutional

bounds. Taking into account the competing interests articulated in *Gerstein*, we believe that a jurisdiction that provides judicial determinations of probable cause within 48 hours of arrest will, as a general matter, comply with the promptness requirement of *Gerstein*. For this reason, such jurisdictions will be immune from systemic challenges.

This is not to say that the probable cause determination in a particular case passes constitutional muster simply because it is provided within 48 hours. Such a hearing may nonetheless violate *Gerstein* if the arrested individual can prove that his or her probable cause determination was delayed unreasonably. Examples of unreasonable delay are delays for the purpose of gathering additional evidence to justify the arrest, a delay motivated by ill will against the arrested individual, or delay for delay's sake. In evaluating whether the delay in a particular case is unreasonable, however, courts must allow a substantial degree of flexibility. Courts cannot ignore the often unavoidable delays in transporting arrested persons from one facility to another, handling late-night bookings where no magistrate is readily available, obtaining the presence of an arresting officer who may be busy processing other suspects or securing the premises of an arrest, and other practical realities.

Where an arrested individual does not receive a probable cause determination within 48 hours, the calculus changes. In such a case, the arrested individual does not bear the burden of proving an unreasonable delay. Rather the burden shifts to the government to demonstrate the existence of a bona fide emergency or other extraordinary circumstance. The fact that in a particular case it may take longer than 48 hours to consolidate pretrial proceedings does not qualify as an extraordinary circumstance. Nor, for that matter, do intervening weekends. A jurisdiction that chooses to offer combined proceedings must do so as soon as is reasonably feasible, but in no event later than 48 hours after arrest.

*McLaughlin, supra,* slip op. at 9-11. The Court held that while the County of Riverside was entitled to combine probable cause determinations with arraignments, their current practices and procedures did not fully comport with the standards articulated above.

# AERIAL SEARCHES

A reasonableness test was also applied to the context of aerial searches in *Florida v. Riley,* 109 S. Ct. 693 (1989). There a Florida officer, following up on an anonymous tip that marijuana was being grown on the property in question, found that the greenhouse on that property was enclosed on two sides, and obscured from view on the other two sides. A wire fence surrounded the defendant's home and the greenhouse, posted with a "do not enter" sign. Since the officer could not see the contents of the greenhouse from the ground because of these factors, he flew over and circled the site in a helicopter, hovering 400 feet above the ground. He used his unaided eyes to look through a space in the roof that partially covered the greenhouse and to look in the open sides. Seeing what appeared to be marijuana growing in the warehouse, the officer then obtained a search warrant. The search, which followed, revealed that marijuana was being grown in the warehouse and the defendant was arrested and charged with possession. The issue raised by this case was whether the results of the search under the warrant should be suppressed as the fruit of a warrantless aerial inspection, which offended constitutional parameters. The Court found the aerial search did not offend constitutional prerogatives, relying upon its 1986 decision in *California v. Ciraolo,* 476 U.S. 207 (1986). There the Court upheld the validity, against a Fourth Amendment challenge, of an aerial search, from a fixed wing plane flying at about 1000 feet, of a garden within the curtilage of a home surrounded by a high privacy fence. The Court held that there was no reasonable expectation of privacy from aerial surveillance of the areas involved in *Riley* and *Ciraolo* from aircraft flying in navigable airspace.

## PLAIN VIEW EXCEPTION TO WARRANT REQUIREMENT

The "plain view exception" to the warrant requirement was the focus of three cases during the period in question. The first of these was *Horton v. California,* 110 S. Ct. 2301 (1990). In this case the officer obtained a valid search warrant for Horton's home to look for proceeds from a robbery, although the affidavit supporting the warrant also described the weapons used by the robbers, The subsequent search of Horton's home did not reveal the proceeds of the robbery, but the officer did find the weapons and other evidence in plain view linking the defendant to the crime. Those items were seized, thereby giving rise to Fourth Amendment implications. Horton was tried and convicted for armed robbery. He sought to suppress the seized evidence on the theory that *it* did not fit within the plain view doctrine articulated by *Collidge v. New Hampshire,* 403 U.s. 443 (1971), because their discovery was not inadvertent. The *Horton* Court expressly rejected the position that inadvertence was a necessary element of the plain view doctrine. It articulated two conditions, which must be satisfied in the context of warrantless plain view seizures. First, the item must both be in plain view and its incriminating nature must be immediately apparent. Second, the officer making the seizure must lawfully be in a location from which the object seized can be plainly seen, and the officer must have lawful access to the object involved itself. In the plain view cases, plain view alone never justified the warrantless seizure of an item. It was always a supplementary justification for the officer's intrusion into the otherwise protected interests. For example, the discovery of the evidence in question might have occurred during execution of a warrant for another object, the discovery may have been made during hot pursuit of a suspect, or it may have occurred during a search incident to an arrest.

In the *Horton* case, the weapons were in plain sight and were clearly of the sort that had been used in the robbery. Therefore, their incriminating nature was immediately apparent. The officer was in the defendant's home pursuant to a valid warrant to search for the proceeds of the robbery; that provided what the Court would term the prior justification. That also formed the basis for the officer to lawfully be in the location where he saw the weapons, and where he had lawful access to them. The *Horton* Court did not feel that an added requirement that the discovery be inadvertent was a necessary part of the plain view doctrine.

In *Illinois v. Rodriguez,* 110 S. Ct. 2793 (1990), the police entered Rodriguez apartment without a warrant. Their entry was based upon the consent of a third party whom the officers believed had common authority over the premises, although the third party in fact did not have such common authority. Upon entering the apartment, the police discovered drug paraphernalia and white powder which the officers believed, correctly, to be cocaine lying in plain view. Rodriguez, who had been asleep in the apartment, was arrested and charged with possession of illegal drugs with intent to dispute.

The Court in the 1974 decision *United States v. Matlock,* 415 U.S. 164 (1974), upheld the warrantless entry and search of a premises by law enforcement officers upon the consent of a third party who had common authority over the premises in question. The *Rodriguez* Court held that the warrantless entry and search based upon the consent of a third party, whom the officers reasonably, though erroneously, believed had common authority over the premises, was constitutionally permissible. Therefore, a plain view seizure based upon such a warrantless entry and search is valid under a

Fourth Amendment analysis, if the belief is reasonable. The *Rodriguez* case was remanded for a determination of whether the belief of the officer in question was reasonable.

## EVIDENCE IN PLAIN VIEW DISCOVERED DURING PROTECTIVE SWEEP OF HOUSE-- SCOPE OF PROTECTIVE SWEEP

The Court's decision in *Maryland v. Buie*, 110 S. Ct. 1093 (1990), also involved a seizure of evidence lying in plain view, but the basis for the entry and search of the premises again differed from those of the previous two cases.

Here, two men, one of whom was wearing a red running suit, committed an armed robbery. The police obtained a valid arrest warrant for Buie which they executed at his house. Buie was arrested emerging from the basement of the home, one of the officers then entered the basement to determine whether there was anyone else there. While in the basement, the officer discovered and seized a red running suit lying in plain view. The issue at bar was what level of justification was required under Fourth Amendment standards before the officer could lawfully enter the basement to determine whether someone else was there. The Court held that the

> Fourth Amendment permits a properly limited protective sweep in conjunction with an in-home arrest when the searching officer possesses a reasonable belief based on specific and articulable facts that the area to be swept harbors an individual posing a danger to those on the arrest scene.

*Id.*, at 1099-1100. A protective sweep is a quick and limited search of a premises incident to an arrest which is conducted to protect the safety of police officers or others. It is limited to a cursory visual inspection of places where persons might be hiding, taking no longer than it takes to complete the arrest and depart the premises. The *Buie* Court holding permits such a protective sweep as a precautionary matter, and the sweep need not be supported by probable cause or reasonable suspicion. However, there must be articulable facts which, taken together with the rational inferences flowing from those facts, would warrant a reasonably prudent officer in believing that the area to be swept harbors an individual posing a threat to those on the arrest scene. *Id.*, at 1098.

In reaching its decision, the *Buie* Court distinguished *Chimel v. California,* 395 U.S. 752 (1969). There, the Court held that, absent a search warrant, the justifiable search incident to an in-home arrest should not extend beyond the arrestee's person and the area from which the arrestee might obtain a weapon. 110 S. Ct., at 1099. The *Chimel* Court was dealing with a detailed "top to bottom" search of the entire house for evidence of the crime with which the defendant was charged. In addition, the focus of the *Chimel* holding was the extent of the justifiable search to prevent a threat to the officers from the arrestee, which in *Buie,* the threat at issue was that posed by third parties in the house. *Id.*

## WARRANTLESS ROUTINE IN-HOME ARREST

The subject of in-home arrests also surfaced in the Court's decision in *New York v. Harris,* 110 S. Ct. 1640 (1990). There the Court expanded upon its decision in *Payton v. New York,* 445 U.S. 573 (1980), where the Court held that the Fourth Amendment prohibits the police from entering a suspect's home without a warrant and without consent in order to make a routine felony arrest. In *Harris,* the Court held that the exclusionary rule does not foreclose the State's use of a written statement made by the defendant at the station house after appropriate *Miranda* warnings, where the defendant had previously been arrested in his home, upon probable cause, in violation of *Payton.* The exclusionary rule did, among other things, foreclose the use of an incriminating statement made by Harris in his home at the time of the arrest, after *Miranda* warnings. The Court emphasized that at the time the station-house statement was made, the defendant was in lawful custody, there having been probable cause to arrest him. The Court saw minimal incremental deterrent benefit to suppressing this statement, noting that under *Payton,* the police know that a warrantless entry will lead to suppression of any evidence found in the home or statements taken inside the home. *Id.,* at 1644-45.

## IMPEACHMENT EXCEPTION TO EXCLUSIONARY RULE

One other case during the time at issue addressed an exclusionary rule issue. In *James v. Illinois,* 110 S. Ct. 648 (1990), the Court considered the possible application of the impeachment exception to the exclusionary rule in a case involving an allegedly warrantless arrest without probable cause. The impeachment exception permits the introduction of illegally obtained evidence for the limited purpose of impeaching the defendant's own testimony. *See, e.g., Oregon v. Hass,* 420 U.S. 714 (1975); *Harris v. New York,* 401 U.S. 222 (1970); *Walder v. United States,* 347 U.S. 62 (1954). In *James,* the Court held that the impeachment exception does not permit the admission of a defendant's illegally obtained prior statement to impeach a defense witness's testimony.

## SEARCHES OF CLOSED CONTAINERS IN VEHICLES

Inventory searches of closed containers in impounded vehicles were the focus of the Court's 1990 decision in *Florida v. Wells,* 110 S. Ct. 1632 (1990). There, the Court found that a policy permitting law enforcement officers some discretion in determining whether to open closed containers during an inventory search of a car, in light of the nature of the search and the characteristics of the container involved, was permissible under Fourth Amendment standards. However, opening such a container in the absence of any policy to assist officers in making the determination whether to open such closed containers encountered during inventory searches was not consistent with Fourth Amendment parameters; any resulting evidence would have to be suppressed.

The Court, in *Florida v. Jimeno,* No. 90-622, slip op. (U.S., May 23, 1991) considered the question of whether the Fourth Amendment was violated by the search of a closed container in a vehicle, where the criminal suspect has given permission to search the car, and the container involved might reasonably hold the object of the search. In this case, a police officer had been following Jimeno's car, after overhearing what appeared to be the arrangement of a drug transaction. While Jimeno was stopped for a routine traffic violation, the officer advised Jimeno that be had reason to believe that Jimeno was carrying drugs in his vehicle and requested permission to search the vehicle. Jimeno *gave* general consent to the search, but did not specifically give permission to search the closed paper bag on the floorboard. The officer opened the bag as part of his search, and found cocaine. Jimeno was charged with possession with intent to distribute cocaine in violation of state law. The trial court had granted Jimeno's motion to suppress the cocaine, and this decision was affirmed on appeal. The U.S. Supreme Court reversed, holding that the "Fourth Amendment is satisfied when, under the circumstances, *it* is objectively reasonable for the officer to believe that the scope of the suspect's consent permitted him to open a particular container within the automobile." *Id.,* slip op. at 1. The Court noted that the "scope of a search is generally defined by its expressed object." *Id.,* at 3. Here the suspect gave the officer permission to search the car without placing any express limitation on the scope of the search; and the suspect knew that the officer would be looking for narcotics in the car, as be had been informed that the officer suspected him of carrying narcotics. The Court concluded that it would be objectively reasonable for the officer to conclude that the general consent was broad enough to include consent to search containers in the car that might hold drugs, such as the paper bag in question. In so doing, the Court distinguished *State v. Wells,* 539 So. 2d 464 (1989), *affd on other grounds sub nom., Florida v. Wells,* 110 S. Ct, 1632 (1990), where the Supreme Court of Florida held that general consent to search a car did not extend to authorization to pry open a locked briefcase which had been found in the trunk of the car. The *Jimeno* Court opined that it was unlikely that a suspect giving such general consent to search the car reasonably expected that consent to include the agreement to break into such a locked container, but distinguished this circumstance from that of a folded paper bag. While the Court acknowledged that a suspect can explicitly limit the scope of his consent, it saw no need to require express permission before a closed container which might reasonably be expected to contain the object of the search could be searched.

Closed containers in vehicles were also the focus of the Court's attention in *California v. Acevedo,* No, 89-1690, slip op. (U.S., May 30, 1991). In this case, police officers observed Acevedo place a closed paper bag in the trunk of his car. The officers had probable cause to believe the paper bag contained marijuana. Fearing that they would lose this evidence, the officers, acting without a warrant, stopped Acevedo, opened the trunk of the car, opened the closed paper bag, and found the marijuana. The matter before the Court was whether the Fourth Amendment in these circumstances required suppression of the marijuana. In analyzing this issue, the Court reviewed its decisions relating to the moving vehicle exception to the warrant requirement under the Fourth Amendment. For example, in *Carroll v. United States,* 267 U.S. 132 (1925), the Court applied this exception, recognizing the exigency that exists because a vehicle can quickly be moved out of the locality or jurisdiction where a warrant must be sought. The *Carroll* Court therefore "held that a warrantless search of an automobile based upon probable cause to believe that the vehicle contained evidence of crime in the light of the exigency arising out of the likely disappearance of the vehicle did not contravene the Warrant Clause of the Fourth Amendment." *Acevedo, supra,* slip op. at 4, *citing Carroll, supra,* 267 U.S., at 158-59. The Court in *Chambers v. Maroney,* 399 U.S. 42 (11970), concluded that one must look to the time at which the vehicle was seized to determine whether exigent circumstances existed. *Chambers* permitted the police to conduct a warrantless search of a vehicle at the police station after the defendant's arrest on the theory that the "police could search later whenever they could have searched earlier, had they so chosen." *Acevedo, supra,* slip op. at 4. In light of the probable cause and exigent circumstances present at the time the vehicle was stopped, a search at the time of the seizure would have passed constitutional muster, and the validity of the later search turned upon what would have been permissible at that time. Thus, "(f)ollowing *Chambers,* if the police have probable cause to justify a warrantless seizure of an automobile on a public roadway, they may conduct either an immediate or a delayed search of the vehicle." *Id.* Under the Court's 1982 decision in *United States v. Ross,* 456 U.S. 798 (1982), "a warrantless search of an automobile under the *Carroll* doctrine could include a search of a container or package found inside the car when such a search was supported by probable cause." *Acevedo, supra,* slip op. at 4-5. The *Ross* Court noted that the scope of a warrantless search based upon probable cause was the same as that of a search supported by a warrant based upon probable cause. 456 U.S., at 823, Applying this to the context of a vehicle search, the Court stated: "If probable cause justifies the search of a lawfully stopped vehicle, it justifies the search of every part of the vehicle and its contents that may conceal the object of the search." *Id.,* at 835. Further, the *Ross* Court distinguished this line of reasoning from the separate rule articulated in its decision in *United States v. Chadwick,* 433 U.S. 1 (1977), and extended by *Arkansas v. Sanders,* 442 U.S. 753 (1979), governing the search of closed containers. 456 U.S., at 817. In those cases, the Court recognized a heightened expectation of privacy in luggage or other personal effects contained in closed containers, which is not diminished by their presence in an automobile. The Court also noted that secure storage facilities are often available when such closed containers are seized. In such circumstances, under *Chadwick* and *Sanders,* absent the suspect's consent to search the closed containers, Fourth Amendment protections were satisfied only when a warrant for the search of the closed containers is obtained.

As applied by *Ross, Carroll* and its progeny controlled those automobile searches where the police have probable cause to search the whole vehicle, while the *Chadwick* doctrine controlled where the police's probable cause extends only to a container in a vehicle. *Acevedo, supra,* slip op. at 6. In the first circumstance, a warrantless search, was constitutionally permissible; while in the second, a warrant had to be obtained. Each search could involve the search of closed containers; the distinction turned not upon the nature of the container, but rather upon the scope of the probable cause supporting the search. In addition, the *Ross* Court rejected the *Chadwick* doctrine's distinction with regard to expectations of privacy in vehicles as opposed to closed containers.

The *Acevedo* Court addressed a question it deemed left open by *Ross,* "whether the Fourth Amendment requires the police to obtain a warrant to open the sack in a movable vehicle simply because they lack probable cause to search the entire car." *Acevedo, supra,* slip op. at 8. The Court concluded that a warrant was not required, overruling the *Chadwick-Sanders* rule, and held that "the Fourth Amendment does not compel separate treatment for an automobile search that extends only to a container within the vehicle." *Id.,* at 10-11. Thus, after *Acevedo:*

> The interpretation of the Carroll doctrine set forth in Ross now applies to all searches of containers found in an automobile. In other words, the police may search without a warrant if their search is supported by probable cause. The Court in Ross put it this way:
>
>> "The scope of a warrantless search of an automobile ... is not defined by the nature of the container in which the contraband is secreted. Rather, it is defined by the object of the search and the places in which there is probable cause to believe that it may be found." 456 U.S., at 824.
>
> It went on to note: "Probable cause to believe that a container placed in the trunk of a taxi contains contraband or evidence does not justify" a search of the entire cab." *Ibid.* We reaffirm that principle. In the case before us, the police had probable cause to believe that the paper bag in the automobile's trunk contained marijuana. That probable cause now allows a warrantless search of the paper bag. The facts in the record reveal that the police did not have probable cause to believe that contraband was hidden in any other part of the automobile and a search of the entire vehicle would have been without probable cause and unreasonable under the Fourth Amendment.

*Acevedo, supra,* slip op. at 14. In so doing, the Court emphasized that it was neither broadening the permissible scope of an automobile search nor extending the *Carroll* doctrine.

## EMPLOYEE DRUG-TESTING

The Court also considered two employee drug-testing cases during the period under review, *Skinner u. Railway Labor Executives Association,* 109 S. Ct. 1402 (1989); and *National Treasury Employees Union v. Von Raab,* 109 S. Ct. 1384 (1989). In *Skinner,* the Court found Fourth Amendment protected privacy interests implicated by the federal regulations requiring employees of private railroads to submit urine samples for drug testing. Similar privacy interests, protected by the Fourth Amendment, were implicated by drug and alcohol testing mandated or authorized under Federal Railroad Administration regulations in *Von Raab.* The Court found these instances where "a Fourth Amendment intrusion serves special governmental needs, beyond the normal need for law enforcement." *Von Raab, supra,* 109 S. Ct., at 1390. In such circumstances, a balancing test is to be applied, balancing the "individual's privacy expectations against the Government's interests to determine whether it is impractical to require a warrant or some level of individualized suspicion in the particular context." *Id.* In both case's the Court found the governmental interests outweighed individual privacy interests, and found the intrusions reasonable under Fourth Amendment standards.

## FOURTH AMENDMENT EXTRA-TERRITORIAL APPLICATION

Finally, in *United States v. Verdugo-Urquidez,* 110 S. Ct. 1056 (1990), the Court determined that the Fourth Amendment had no extraterritorial application to searches or seizures, by United States agents, of property owned by a non-resident alien, where that property was located in a foreign country.

## CONCLUSIONS

In its 1988, 1989, and 1990 Terms, the Supreme Court has been extremely active in the Fourth Amendment field. There appears to be a general narrowing of the sweep of the Fourth Amendment, although some areas remain sacrosanct. The standards and tests applied by the Court vary somewhat depending upon context. In evaluating the case law and trends in this area, sensitivity is required to the delicate balance between the needs of legitimate law enforcement efforts and the need to protect the privacy and property interests of the individual against unlawful or abusive incursions into those protected rights. The Court's recent decisions suggest adherence to the principle that, in general, warrantless searches are per se unreasonable under Fourth Amendment standards, unless such searches fall within one of the exceptions to the warrant requirement. The Court's recent activity has been largely focused upon the nature and scope of those exceptions.

# INDEX

## A

access to student records, 12
actual damages, 18, 23
aerial searches, 52, 53, 65
alleged violation, 19, 23
ambiguity, vii, 1
American culture, 1
anonymous, 2, 36, 54, 55, 66
arrest records, 4
articulable facts, 54-56, 68
Attorney General, 18-20, 24, 30, 42
Automated Personal Data Systems, 5, 6, 8, 9, 35

## B

bank records, 14, 15
Bank Secrecy Act, 13, 14
Bill of Rights, vii, 2, 4
Border Patrol, 58
Buckley Amendment, 12

## C

Cable Communications Policy Act, 18
California v. Acevedo, 71
California v. Ciraolo, 66
Carroll v. United States, 71
Carter Administration, 10, 13, 30
Carter, President James, 9, 10
Chambers v. Maroney, 72
checkpoints, 52, 53, 58
Chief Information Officer of the United States (CIOUS), 31
children, 12, 26
Children's Online Privacy Protection Act (COPPA), 26
Chimel v. California, 69
civil action, 18-20, 23, 24
Clinton Administration, 25, 26, 30, 32, 41, 46
Clinton, President, 40, 44, 47
closed container, 70
cocaine, 55, 60, 67, 70
Code of Fair Information Practice, 6, 35
compliance, 11, 14
Computer Matching and Privacy Protection Act, 21
computer matching, 21, 22, 33
Computer Security Act, 21
Constitution, 1, 17, 41, 52, 64
constitutionality, 59
County of Riverside v. McLaughlin, 64
Crime Control Act, 7
criminal activity, 17, 54-56, 58, 59

customer transactions, 13

## D

Data Privacy Directive, 36
deadly force, 61, 62
direct mail marketing, 27
disclosure, 2, 7, 8, 11, 12, 23, 26, 27, 37-41
Driver's Privacy Protection Act (DPPA), 23, 24
drug and alcohol testing, 74
Drug Enforcement Administration (DEA), 55
drug testing, 52, 53, 74
duplicate records, 13

## E

eavesdropping, 3
electronic commerce, 44, 48
electronic communication, 19, 20
Electronic Communications Privacy Act (ECPA), 18-20
Electronic Funds Transfer (EFT), 14
electronic signature, 26, 37, 44, 45
Electronic Signatures in Global and National Commerce Act (E-SIGN), 45
e-mail marketing, 27
encoding, 46
encryption, 36, 46, 48
European Community, 28
European Union (EU), 28, 36
excessive force, 52, 60, 62, 63
expectation of privacy, 53, 72
expectation, 1, 15, 59, 66

## F

Fair Credit Reporting Act, 6, 7
Family Educational Rights and Privacy Act (FERPA), 12, 48
federal benefits, 22, 33

Federal Bureau of Investigation (FBI), 20, 41, 42
Federal Communications Commission, 44, 46
federal criminal code, 19, 20
federal funds, 12
Federal Government, 11, 31, 32
Federal Trade Commission, 26, 27, 34, 42
Fifth Amendment, 2
financial assistance, 22
financial institution, 14, 16
financial privacy, 14, 15
financial records, 13, 14, 16
First Amendment, 2, 7, 17, 44, 46
Florida v. Bostick, 56
Florida v. Jimeno, 70
Ford Administration, 30
Foreign Intelligence Surveillance Act, 20
foreign policy, 21
fraud, 22, 30, 33, 38, 46

## G

General Education Provisions Act, 12
Gerstein v. Pugh, 64
Government Paperwork Elimination Act (GPEA), 45
Gramm-Leach-Bliley Act, 27, 33
grand jury subpoena, 12, 23

## H

Harvard Law Review, 2
Health and Human Services (HHS), 22, 25, 36
health care, 25, 35-39, 41
Health Insurance Portability and Accountability Act (HIPAA), 25, 36, 38
health insurance, 25
Horton v. California, 53, 66
hot pursuit, 67

# Index

## I

identifiable information, 8, 18, 33, 39, 43
identification, 25, 36, 54, 56, 58, 59
Identity Theft and Assumption Deterrence Act, 41
illegal activity, 58
Illinois v. Rodriguez, 67
impeachment, 52, 70
individual rights, 5
inferences, 54, 68
information technology (IT), 21, 32, 35
intelligence, 19, 21, 35
interception, 19, 42
Interest Rate Control Act, 16
interference, 59
internet, 8, 26, 31, 41-44, 46-48
interpretation, 73
invasion of privacy, 3, 4, 34
invasion, 41, 45, 46
investigatory stop, 52, 54, 55, 62, 63

## J

James v. Illinois, 69
Johnson v. Glick, 63
justification, 22, 57, 67, 68

## K

knowledge, 30

## L

law enforcement, 7, 12, 16, 17, 20, 22, 23, 35, 38-40, 42, 43, 46, 53, 62, 67, 70, 74, 75
legal status, 44
legislation, 6, 9, 13, 18, 28, 30, 31, 34, 37, 38, 40-42, 44, 47
litigation costs, 18, 23

Locke, John, 1, 2
luggage, 56, 72

## M

marijuana, 55, 66, 71, 73
medical records legislation, 35
medical records, 26, 34-40
Members of Congress, 42
Mexico, 58
Miami, 56
military personnel, 33
Miranda warnings, 69
money laundering, 34
money, 14, 34

## N

narcotics, 56, 71
National Institute of Standards and Technology (NIST), 21
National Research Council, 35
national security, 30, 46
new technology, 2, 3, 42
New York v. Harris, 53, 69
Ninth Amendment, 2
non-resident alien, 74

## O

Office of Information and Regulatory Affairs (OIRA), 10, 28, 30, 45
Office of Management and Budget (OMB), 8, 10, 11, 22, 29, 31, 43-45
Omnibus Consolidated and Emergency Supplemental Appropriations Act, 26, 45
online privacy protections, 8, 43

## P

Paperwork Reduction Act, 10, 11

Payton v. New York, 69
personal data systems, 5, 6
personal health information, 35, 38, 40
personal information, 48
personally identifiable information, 8, 18, 32, 33, 39, 43
plain view exception, 66
plain view seizures, 67
police, 17, 46, 54-57, 59-61, 63, 67-73
possession with intent to distribute, 70
principle, 73, 75
Privacy Commission Act, 29
privacy expectations, 2, 53, 74
privacy legislation, 26, 30, 37
Privacy Protection Act, 17, 21, 23, 26, 41
Privacy Protection Study Commission, 8-10, 12-14, 16, 28-30, 35
private homes, vii, 2
private sector, 9, 13, 31, 44
proposals, 10, 11, 29, 34, 47
public health, 38, 39
public interest, 59
public opposition, 34
public policy, 39
punishment, 62, 63
punitive damages, 6, 18, 23

## R

reasonable suspicion, 54-60, 68
recognition, vii, 2
reliability, 54, 55
response, 9, 24, 26, 41, 43
retrieval, iv, 44
Right of Privacy, 3, 30
Right to Financial Privacy Act (RFPA), 10, 13, 14, 16
right to privacy, 2

## S

Secretary of the Treasury, 27, 34
security measures, 37
seized, 51, 54, 57, 60, 66, 68, 72
self-employed, 25
self-incrimination, vii, 2
self-regulation, 28, 41
Senate, 3, 4, 12, 37, 38-40, 47
sobriety checkpoint, 58
Social Security number, 5, 47
State v. Wells, 71
statistics, 11
subpoena, 12, 15, 16, 17, 30
suppression, 69, 71
Supreme Court, 2, 14, 15, 17, 23, 24, 51, 52, 56-58, 60, 61, 63, 70, 74
suspicious transactions, 34

## T

tax revenues, 14
taxes, 14
technologically secure environment, 36
technology, 14, 18, 32, 45, 48
Telecommunications Act, 24
telecommunications, 14, 24, 44
telemarketing, 27
Telephone Consumer Protection Act, 46
Tennessee v. Garner, 61
theory, 60, 66, 72
Third Amendment, 2
third parties, 8, 17, 27, 31, 43, 69
threat, 14, 61-63, 68, 69
troops, vii, 2

## U

unauthorized access, 21, 26, 36, 37
United Kingdom, 3
United States, 7, 10, 14, 16, 28, 36, 52-55, 58, 74

unreasonable searches and seizures, 15, 51, 52
Unsolicited Commercial Electronic Mail (UCE), 46, 48

## V

validity, 66, 72
Video Privacy Protection Act, 23
violence, 62
Violent Crime Control and Law Enforcement Act, 23

voluntary submission, 43

## W

Walder v. United States, 70
warrantless search, 72, 73
warrantless, 52, 54, 64, 66, 67, 69-71, 73, 75
warrants, 17, 51, 52
wire interception, 3
wiretap program, 42
wrongdoing, 53, 54, 60